HEALING THE FRACTURED SELF

Jack Walters

THE SEABURY PRESS

Cover design: Art Direction, Inc.

Printed in the United States of America

Although the case histories contained in this book are based on actual cases from the author's practice, care has been taken to disguise incidental details of personal history. Any resemblance, therefore, to any person, living or dead, on the part of any of the patients in this book, is purely coincidental and was not intended by the author.

Library of Congress Catalog Card Number: 83-20092

ISBN: 0-86683-883-X

5 4 3 2 1

Winston Press, Inc.
430 Oak Grove
Minneapolis, Minnesota 55403

To Fred

CONTENTS

Part I

THE INTERNAL DIALOGUE

1

INTRODUCTORY NOTE

Some years ago, as I sat listening to a patient talk about her sense of isolation and immobilization, I began to become aware of the way she referred to herself. It sounded as though she was an outsider—another person. She'd say, "You have to clean the house today!" or "You'd better do the shopping!" When I asked her about this, she explained, "When I hear those commands, I dig my heels in and don't get anything done!" She did not refer to herself in the first person: "I" want to do the cleaning or "I" want to do the shopping; moreover, it sounded as though she was being ordered around from within herself by another: an unseen but powerful speaker. She herself described it as a rebellion going on inside.

I wondered if she was conscious of the way she referred to herself. At first she was puzzled by my observation. But, with the help of my tape recorder, I was able to replay those parts of our conversation. She listened. When the playback ended, I asked her to describe what had been going on inside of her each time she used "you" instead of "I." She paused a moment to think, then smiled wryly. "The 'you' . . . it's like a stern voice in my head yelling at me," she said. "It's a voice that commands me at every turn and makes decisions as to what to do, what to feel, and who to be. It's this voice I'm constantly battling."

It seemed that there was more here than an individual's quirk, and my hunch paid off. I began listening to others for the same or similar speech patterns, and soon discovered that they are shared by a number of people. Significantly, they seemed to agree with each other in their perceptions of the cause: "It's like a voice inside my head talking to me." I explored the patterns further and found that these "inner voices" did more than talk.

More often than not the tone of these "voices" was demanding, mean-spirited, and abusive. Most of us have experienced the phenomenon of *talking to ourselves.* For some, however, the effects have dire consequences. Those who are most severely controlled by "inner voices" suffer debilitating psychological as well as physiological symptoms: profound depression; a sense of inner void and worthlessness; physical immobilization; anxiety; the compulsion to overwork; alcoholism; drug abuse; isolation; fear of relationships; a recognizable pattern in the breakdown of relationships; and a wide range of physical disorders including stomach and intestinal disorders, chronic muscular tension, particularly of the neck and shoulders, headaches, and a high susceptibility to colds and other infections. But more significantly, these people experience a severely impoverished quality of life: a radical sense of being outside of the mainstream of the nourishing existence that others enjoy.

While it's important to present a clear picture of this internal struggle as I've seen it, it's just as important to me to recreate the sense of drama involved when a person becomes conscious of this struggle and attempts to deal with it. Above all, I want to avoid becoming locked in technical jargon and abstract theory. To reap the benefits of both, so to speak, this book is structured around the histories of two former patients, Dana and Chris, who suffered considerably in response to these inner voices. Wherever possible, I have incorporated transcripts of their sessions into the text.

While we might understand and sympathize with Dana and Chris, we could dismiss them as unique: as individuals who were suffering from conditions peculiar to them. I do not find that to be true, though. When listening carefully to most people, I find that the substitution of "you" for "I" is incredibly common. Furthermore, when I explore the deeper significance of this with those who have just used it, their responses are strikingly similar. So, while Dana and Chris provide the real-life experiences which come about as a result of this struggle, in the end it's important to remember that they are prototypes and represent similar conditions in each of us which vary from person to person, from history to history.

When Dana and Chris first approached me, they were both locked in internal conflicts. However, their psychological reactions differed in significant ways. It's for this reason that I've selected Dana and Chris; because, while they were both dealing with a very similar kind of internal process, their different responses in reaction to their own internal voices offer us a clear picture of the many avenues available to the Self in its struggle against the dictates of the internal monitor. Both Dana and Chris suffered from a great deal of psychological pain, and both of them, with a great deal of effort, courage, and an increased understanding and appreciation of their conflicts, successfully traveled the road to psychological health.

This book is the result of the many years I spent in an effort to penetrate and understand the causative processes behind this struggle: "the battle within." When and how does this phenomenon begin in most people? What steps can be taken to defuse the incredible and seemingly awesome power that these "inner voices" exert over the will of the Self?

It's been my hope that Dana and Chris's success would encourage others. Maybe within these pages lies the inspiration for you to take steps to defuse the power of your own internal monitor. Dana and Chris discovered that psychological autonomy *can* be attained, and they learned that, once they succeeded in winning out over their "internal authority," they were then able to have a comfortable interpersonal relationship—something they had desired for a long time. Their journey toward self-discovery mirrors that desire in all of us: a passionate urge to come to grips with our own realities. So maybe, just maybe, these stories will ignite that urge in you and propel you on your own journey into "the heart of darkness" and out again into the assurance and warmth of self-discovery.

This is not, however, a self-help book. It is not designed as a substitute for psychiatric or professional psychotherapeutic help if the person seeking this help is severely depressed, anxious, or isolated because of severe interpersonal difficulties. On the one hand, there are kinds of depression and anxiety which seem to be rooted in a person's given biological makeup. Physiological symptoms can only be treated biochemically, that is, with medication. The function of medical psychiatry is to determine whether a person is suffering from a chemical (medical) imbalance and should be treated with medication. Ironically, a person suffering from such a chemical imbalance could receive a lifetime of psychotherapy and experience little or no alleviation of the initial depression or anxiety; rather than mitigating these symptoms, psychotherapy could exacerbate them.

On the other hand, there are symptoms of depression, anxiety, and difficulties in interpersonal relating which are the result of the individual's psychological development as a child. This type of depression, for example, usually arises out of a problem or conflict based on the individual's own value system, but the crux of the difficulty, which usually eludes the person, is that this personal value system is based on false concepts and inaccurate perceptions of Self and the interpersonal world. In most instances these false concepts and inaccurate perceptions are rooted in the kind of messages frequently communicated to the child by a parental figure; however, at other times, by virtue of its circumstances, the child's interpretation of an event may have a special internal significance which bears little or no connection to the real event.

In such a case, it's the child's subjective interpretation of an event and the parental message which becomes the basis of an erroneous assumption. Early in my training, a patient related an event of special significance in her life and in so doing offered me a concrete insight into how this process unfolds. She was about 18 months old when her mother (then a young woman herself) contracted hepatitis. Unfortunately, the mother had no one to turn to in this emergency, so, when she was hospitalized, the child was placed in an orphanage. The same child as an adult interpreted her being placed in an orphanage by her mother as nothing less than her mother's rejection of her. This was far from her mother's intention. Yet without a doubt she perceived this event as one of maternal rejection and abandonment and subsequently integrated this distorted perception into her internal reality. Unfortunately, no matter what the parent's intention, if a child attributes to a parental action a negative message about itself and its interpersonal world—largely if not totally unfounded in the real event—the child, and ultimately the child as an adult, carries this distortion inside itself and uses it as the basis on which it makes decisions about its life.

A common distorted message perceived by a child is that, as an individual, it possesses no innate value *until* or *unless* the parent confers value upon it. A message like this might be communicated subtly, through a parent's not verbalizing love for the child unless the child behaves in a way that merits parental approval. The child's sense of value and worth become totally dependent on "good" behavior, the standard of good being set up for the child by the parent. It then follows in the mind of the child that it is worthless, or—worse yet—not lovable in and of itself. It has to struggle continuously to win worth for itself by behaving as others would want it to. This, of course, is nonsense. Every human being has intrinsic worth regardless of what other people think. But if the child and later the adult believes that its worth and value as a human being comes from an outside source, then a sense of worthlessness and a psychologically based anxiety or depression growing out of this assumption will pervade every aspect of its life.

Psychotherapy is equipped to help the person who suffers from *this* kind of anxiety or depression to examine assumptions like these, so that the internal values which these misconceptions spawn can be let go and new ones brought to realization.

However, some disorders are a combination of both a psychiatric and psychological dysfunction. Many patients I've worked with have suffered from both, and, in an overwhelming majority of cases, no psychotherapeutic progress was possible until the chemical dysfunction was treated. Dana is an example of a patient who had problems because of psychiatric and psychological dysfunctions. There are extremely complex processes at work, and the scope of the complexity looms when we consider that most psychological processes at the root of severe pain are by and large unconscious and therefore unavailable to the subject. Consider too that these unconscious processes might lie in wait, ready to ambush. The effects of such attacks might not be as apparent as we'd suspect. A complete physical or psychological breakdown would be quite obvious, but a mild case of the jitters or a passing "blue" period that turns into continuous anxiety or depression may go unnoticed.

This book is about two people and their struggle to come to terms with their own dysfunctional and unconscious beliefs about themselves and others. That struggle involved digging down deep into the unconscious of each, using tools that were observable and available to us: the words they used; their interactions with others; their posture and behavior in different settings. These clues allowed us to get at the underlying unconscious content that ruled their lives.

This book (or any other book) is no substitute for professional help; but it can increase our awareness of our internal lives and, more specifically, of the internal dialogue in which most of us engage. If you end up realizing that there is a very powerful internal speaker making demands on you through a set of assumptions—if you end up realizing that there are definite ways in which this speaker manifests itself and, through these manifestations, you're able to change the course of the dialogue and the virtual slavery it burdens you with, then you're in a much better position to control your life and direct it in those areas you find the most satisfying and rewarding.

Unfortunately, my experience in lectures and workshops has shown me that many people, just moments after hearing the core of this material and recognizing the patterns and the harmful effects of this internal process in their own lives, unknowingly return to the same patterns, patterns which moments before they intellectually recognized as destructive. Obviously, the intellectual understanding they gained wasn't enough to control or change these processes. In my practice I began to appreciate the great deal of time and psychotherapeutic input it takes to help people develop a well-integrated skill of self-observation. It's in this self-observation that we can come to apply what we understand intellectually and can thereby free ourselves from that very powerful inner process which keeps us so bound-up inside ourselves. The step between intellectually understanding the process and observing it when it manifests itself in behavior is an essential one and to bridge it most people need a guide: someone outside of them, someone not involved in their struggles, who can be objective, mirroring verbal cues and overt behavior that signal the presence of an underlying unconscious process.

I hope to lay the foundation so that you can take your very first steps toward being yourself. By recognizing that this damaging internal dialogue exists in you, you can take your first step to freedom. Many of you will find that what is described in this book makes sense and rings a loud bell of recognition. Still you may find that the process continues unabated inside you. Remember, it's an unconscious process for the most part, so its moves are subtle. More often than not, such subtlety isn't recognized unless observed by an objective and trained expert. This book can be used as a tool in recognizing this process, but it's only one of the many tools available and *necessary* if the complexity of the process is to be dealt with effectively and lastingly. If anyone believes that it only takes a hammer to build a house, well, we recognize immediately how foolish such a belief is. But that belief must be compared to a mistaken attitude towards this book: like the hammer, it's a start, but not the final solution.

2

THE INTERNAL CHARACTERS

The Conversation

The conversation between Dana and me that follows may serve as a starting point in understanding the internal dialogue: how it works and specifically how it undermines healthy attitudes and so becomes the root of a great deal of psychological pain and upheaval.

Jack: You're saying "It's hard for me to get myself to do things sometimes." What's that like?

Dana: Well . . . this morning, for example—I didn't feel well when I first got up. But I ate breakfast, walked the dog . . . then I threw up my breakfast. So, I went back to bed for about half an hour. But that didn't help, so I took some medicine and then went back to bed. After a while I started feeling better, but before I could move it took about fifteen minutes of lying there and telling myself "You're going to get up now and mist all your plants!" [She says this in a demanding tone.] It took me a good fifteen minutes to get my forces marshalled so I could get up and mist my plants.

Jack: Okay. Now, what was the process that took place during those fifteen minutes? Can you describe what was going on inside your head?

Dana: Well, I'd lie there and then look up at the clock. I'd ask myself "Can I get up yet?" And this morning the answer was "No, I can't get up now, but I'm going to get up in fifteen minutes. I'm going to give myself fifteen minutes more to lie here, and then I'll get up." Then the question came: "After I get up, what am I going to do?" So I lie there and list in my head all the things I could do, like mist the plants or write some letters. Then I have to find out which of these things I *can* do.

Jack: What do you mean by "can do"?

Dana: It's just that . . . um . . . I have a few letters to write and I *have* to write them before the end of the week. There's no specific deadline; they just have to be written before the end of the week. I don't *have* to do them today. I don't *have* to do them tomorrow. But, when the thought of choosing between today and tomorrow comes into my head . . . I know that I wouldn't get out of bed if I decided to write those letters today. I'd continue to lie there rather than write those letters.

Jack: How did you know that?

Dana: I just did . . . A kinda sinking feeling in my stomach . . . I really . . . I can't write the letters . . . [her voice has changed and become soft and pleading like that of a child]. I don't know why I reacted, "I can't write the letters." I just couldn't. I wanted to do something that wouldn't require thought or concentration . . . just kinda play with my plants, cut off dead leaves, rearrange the wood chips in the bottom of the pots. You know, that kind of thing. I just wanted to putter with my hands. So, that's what I did, but . . . [she hesitates]. The trouble is that on days like this I don't seem to know what my true desires and needs are. I don't *know* what I want to do.

"You're going to get up now and mist the plants!" That was my clue. Notwithstanding its subtlety and brevity it was clear that during my conversation with Dana the voice of another person emerged. Superficially, the switch from "I" to "you" could be described as a common idiom when a person talks to himself. When alerted to this switch, most people relate it to a means of self-observation; in other words, this internal dialogue is a process whereby the individual can play out various roles, weigh different values and deal with important conflicts. But this explanation doesn't take into account two important facets of the switching from "I" to "you."

First, if Dana were simply speaking with herself on this occasion, why did she use "I" in some instances and "you" in others? If this is simply a means of evaluation for the individual, then the "you" reference is not necessary when another person is present. In this particular instance it would have been just as easy for Dana to say "I'm going to get up and mist my plants." The use of "you" then becomes a point of separation as it is in normal exchanges between two people. *I am/you are* are phrases which identify; they serve to separate the subject ("I") from others ("you"). So, when Dana hears—or, for that matter, when we hear Dana recall— "You're going to get up and mist the plants!" we are hearing the voice of a person separate and distinct from Dana.

The second point concerns tone, because, in addition to the change from "I" to "you," there is a change in voice tone. For example, when Dana asks herself "Can I get up yet?" her reply is "No, I can't get up yet. I'm going to give myself fifteen minutes more." Her reply is consistent. In a matter of seconds this changes. When Dana addresses herself with "you," her tone becomes harsh and overbearing. "You're going to get up now and mist your plants!" Dana recalls these words in the demanding tone in which she heard them.

These combined factors pointed to disparate elements in Dana's inner relating. These portions of my conversation with Dana indicated that I was hearing more than the convenient use of simple idiom. From then on I started to appreciate the presence of another speaker—formidable but subtle—internalized in Dana's psyche but as separate from Dana's Self as Dana is separate from any other human being who might be watching, judging, criticizing, or even threatening her. It was important for Dana to appreciate this as well, so I replayed the tape of that exchange. When we heard it again, I began to explore the shift from "I" to "you" with her.

Jack: Can you tell me what happened when you said: "But before I could move, it took about fifteen minutes of lying there and telling myself 'You're going to get up and mist all your plants'"? Did you notice that you started out with "I could move . . ." but then shifted to "You're going to . . ."? Can you tell me what happened there?

Dana: [Smiling.] Yes. It's like there's a voice inside of me telling me what to do. It sounds very harsh and judgmental when I hear it.

Jack: Well, when I heard it, it sounded very harsh but at another point you asked yourself "Can I get up yet?" and answered with "I." "No, I can't get up yet but I'm going to get up in fifteen minutes . . ." etc. Can you tell me what happened there?

Dana: [She thinks a while.] There are two voices in my head. It's like there are two parts to me. [She pauses.]

Jack: What happened with those two parts this morning?

Dana: [There's a brief moment of silence.] One part of me just wanted to relax. The other part told me that I had all these things that had to be done. The more this part demanded, the more the first part rebelled. But the part that rebels isn't strong. It tries to hold out against a flood of demands that other part makes, but I end up getting squeezed between them. I end by being immobilized by them because I don't know what to do. I can't make a decision.

For the first time Dana was hearing the parts that had been speaking to her day in and day out. I heard them too; as clearly as if another person were doing the talking. In fact, the parts which Dana refers to are internal persons who have characteristics and existences quite real and distinct unto themselves. While these inner persons cannot be seen, they are heard, and the effects of the ongoing relationships with them can be consciously experienced and acknowledged. I'm sure most of us have heard the voices of our internal persons. But the key lies in dealing with them as real entities that can and usually do exert tremendous pressure on the will. These inner persons must be acknowledged before we can challenge their positions of control. And there's no doubt that these internal persons control!

My suspicions about a set of internal persons who were interacting with Dana and each other were confirmed by Dana herself. But it was also becoming clearer that the debilitating and violent nature of Dana's ailments (her vomiting, diarrhea, and colitis) and her psychological immobilization were Dana's reaction to these internal persons, who were exercising tremendous power over her. One part of Dana had discovered that these symptoms offered her a means of resisting the stringent demands of these internal persons. Specifically, Dana's lethargy and illness became a way in which she could fight this antagonist inside her even though in the long run it was a desperate and self-destructive way of resisting.

While Dana maintained relationships with human beings in the real world, she also interacted and related to internal persons in her own psychic world. Her relationships with these internal persons were as intense as were her relationships with others like her husband and me. Moreover, the dynamics of the daily relating Dana maintained with these internal persons followed patterns that are recognizable in external relationships between members of a close-knit group such as a family. It became important to help Dana not only recognize the internal dialogue but also acknowledge the *real presence* of these people. By identifying and acknowledging the reality of these persons Dana could confront them and what they represented.

We had discovered the presence of real persons in Dana's psyche. We heard what they said, we saw the disastrous effects that occurred when Dana interacted with them. But we hadn't named them as yet. Who were these internal persons who spoke to Dana with such truculent force? What were their origins?

Naming the Speaker

A primary need of the human being is to be in contact with other human beings. In infancy this need is fulfilled by the mother's physical presence: her care and affection for the child. As the little one moves from the passive state of infancy into childhood, it is compelled to seek active ways of satisfying the need for human contact. The first initiative the child assumes in this direction is to copy surrounding adults, usually its parents, but also other influential "parental" figures such as a grandparent, an aunt or uncle, or an older sibling. The child feels pleasure when it successfully mimics adults. In a later stage of development we can easily observe the child's delight when it has mirrored the hand movements of an adult in a game like "patty cake." A child learns by imitating, and the self-satisfaction the child experiences when it is able to use and control yet another mental or physical facility is one part of the impetus to imitate. But, more significantly, the child covets the approval and acceptance of the parent, which is the highest prize in the child's eyes for successful mimicry. That is the child's experience of being loved by the other.

Beginning around the age of two-and-one-half, a psychic process begins in the child's mind. At this time the child has at its disposal a psychological tool which helps it cope with the boundaries and rules that the parent sets for it. The child is now capable of using the parent as a model from which it constructs an internalized image of that parent: namely, behavior prohibited by as well as behavior acceptable to the parent. By using this image, the child can, in its own mind, protect itself from the loss of love or guarantee the ongoing love of the parent.

At the same time, the child's interest in fairy tales is heightened because in fairy tales through the imagery of the story the child is working out this internal process. In most fairy tales the scenario runs along these lines: an innocent child whose good parent has died, disappeared, or been taken ill, is confronted by a wicked witch (the image of the vitriolic, overpowering parent) who makes unrelenting and impossible demands on the child. When the child fails to meet these demands, which are always beyond its reach, the witch threatens it with some terrible punishment like the destruction of something the child loves dearly, imprisonment, or death. But in the end the child manages to escape the evil clutches of the witch by outwitting, overpowering, or killing it—usually through the aid of a good fairy (the image of the kind, accepting parent) who has given the child a magic formula or secret device for attaining freedom. These elements are found in the best-known fairy tales of western literature. While hundreds exist, "Snow White," "Hansel and Gretel," "Cinderella," "The Wizard of Oz," and "Rumplestiltskin" readily come to mind. These fairy tales and others like them provide insight into a child's emerging psychic process.

Inherent in the child's internal process are conflicts revolving around a child's fear of inadequacy in the face of parental demands. At this point, it is not unusual for the child to seek help from the "good" parent to meet the "bad" parent's demands, but the "good" parent is not always available to help the child through each and every predicament that may arise. So the child relies on the images of the "good" and "bad" parent which it has internalized in its psyche to monitor its behavior. The threatening parental image alerts the child to a potential transgression. The image of the accepting parent, whom the child wants to please, stands by the child to encourage good behavior. If the child transgresses, the threatening parental image verbally reproaches the child and warns of more severe punishment if the forbidden act is repeated. Thus, this image acts as an early warning system in which the anxiety that is generated in the child is similar to flashing lights and the ringing of alarm bells. Often a child will say, "Mommy won't like you if you do that again." To the child the severe punishment is the loss of the approval of the loving and accepting parent.

At this stage the child's behavior is still oriented toward adult approval but this behavior has grown more complex. Eavesdropping on an exchange between a three-year-old and its favorite doll, teddy bear, or imaginary playmate might permit us to hear something like: "You've been a naughty girl!" or "You're a nice teddy bear." Very often the child will strike the doll if the child itself has misbehaved. I recall an example of this kind of child behavior that occurred not too long ago. One afternoon I was entertaining several couples and their children in my home. Jane, one of the mothers, was very anxious about the activity and whereabouts of her four-year-old daughter Mary, who was busily exploring my very large apartment. Every few minutes Jane would send her husband or one of the older children down the hall to check on Mary. I tried to assure Jane that the other rooms in the apartment were occupied at the time so Mary wouldn't be completely unattended wherever she was. Still, Jane couldn't relax until Mary came back into the room with us and settled down at the coffee table with a felt-tipped pen and a piece of paper. Mary drew quietly until, in an attempt to make dots, she began to use the pen in a way that would destroy the tip. Since it was my pen and I didn't want it ruined, I quietly asked Mary if she wouldn't use the pen that way. Before I could say another word, Jane interrupted and in a sharp tone of voice said "Mary! Don't do that." Mary's look of wounded surprise quickly changed to anger. If looks could kill. . . . Not more than a minute later, Mary took hold of her doll. She rolled up the sheet of paper and stuck it in the doll's mouth. She then slapped the doll and mimicked her mother's words: "Don't do that! Don't do that! You bad girl!"

Needless to say, our attention shifted back to Mary. Jane explained that this wasn't unusual behavior for her. Although her dolls seemed to be very important to her and she showered them with much concern and care, it was not unusual for Mary to hit or spank them. By attributing the bad behavior to her doll, Mary had psychologically disowned the action that caused her mother's disapproval. By disowning the action, Mary created a psychological vacuum which was instantly filled by Mary's internalized image of the disapproving parent. Mary's compulsion to punish her doll for her own behavior as well as her taking the verbal role of her mother showed that she had internalized the parental image projected by Jane's patterned reaction to her. At the same time, Mary was disowning herself as a playing child by projecting that part of herself onto the doll.

Interestingly and more significantly, the message that Mary got from her interaction with her mother that afternoon, I suspect, had nothing to do with the proper use of the pen. Mary scolded her doll in response to the rolled up paper and not in response to the use of the pen. All afternoon Jane's interaction with her daughter was based on her desire to maintain control of her child. This, of course, had put Mary's spontaneous activity under close scrutiny. Jane's compulsion to monitor Mary at all times during that afternoon and habitually at other times communicated to Mary that spontaneity itself was the cause of parental disapproval.

If we could go back fifty years and observe Dana's interactions with her parents, we probably would have seen a similar process. Notwithstanding the boundaries of time, we *can* observe similar scenarios in the present in Dana's adult behavior. Just as Mary implanted her mother's image within her psyche that afternoon in my apartment, so too when Dana was a little girl she internalized her perceptions of her parents and these images became fixed in her psyche and continued to exert a profound influence over Dana's psychological being. If you will, psychological time for Dana stopped years ago. Socially and biologically she was a responsible adult female. Psychologically, however, she was still that small child interacting with her parental images and limited to the spectrum of feelings and thoughts that existed in the child-parent relationship—and, in Dana's case, a severely delimiting relationship too!

The internal speaker was able to wield so much influence and power over Dana's life partly because Dana never recognized it as a separate entity apart from herself. It never occurred to her that this source of conflict might not be a part of herself, or that when she heard this internal speaker, she was hearing the dictates of another—a psychological entity as distinct from her as any other human being—and so she treated this entity as a part of herself.

As long as this speaker remained nameless, she couldn't begin to appreciate its effect on her life or hope to break away from its power. Dana needed to identify the speaker, and the first step in identification is naming. By naming this demanding and destructive entity Dana could begin to direct at this elusive dictator a great deal of the hostility and anger which she normally aimed at herself. By drawing upon her present behavior, her immediate concerns and problems, and her developmental psychological history, we were able to discern patterns. In fact, we found ourselves usually working backwards from a particular conflict. Dana would then articulate the message from the internal speaker as it concerned the conflict. Soon enough the messages began to strike notes and tones of familiarity in Dana's history, and before long we were able to name the speaker. It was Dana's Internal Parent, or "Inner Other." (The term "Internal Parent" has been the one I have used in the past with my patients, but I have decided in this book to substitute for it the term "Inner Other." Although historically most people's Inner Others are formed in response to parental admonitions, it is not only parents who discipline children. Other older relatives, older siblings, teachers, clergy, and other authority figures can all help in forming a person's Inner Other. In addition, the term "Internal Parent" can be easily confused with the "Parent" of Transactional Analysis, though in fact there are significant differences between them. In this book, therefore, I have decided to use the term "Inner Other" to designate that internalized function of admonition, suppression, and control which is opposed to the ego or Central "I.")

This psychological process which grew out of Dana's history is not peculiar to Dana. If anything, we are dealing with a process that evidence shows to be universal. The intensity of the dialogue that goes on between subject and Inner Other varies from individual to individual, but regardless of intensity the exchange between subject and Inner Other exists in all of humanity. In our century, especially since Freud, we've come to understand this as a psychological phenomenon, and all eminent psychologists agree that this process in varying degrees occurs in all humans. However, long before Freud and the appearance of modern psychological jargon that our age has borne and nurtured, the process was understood and explained in folklore and religious mythologies. Folklore tales involving witches, evil queens and evil kings, dragons, princesses, giants—all of these images assisted in the working out of the deep, dark, and profound conflicts common to all people within the framework of a story. Within the context of this form the inner speaker might be the Inner Witch.

Not only Dana and a select few experience the debilitating psychological dysfunction caused by virtual subjugation to these dark inner forces; all of us experience it to a greater or lesser degree. It is vital that we all acknowledge the reality of these inner forces and the dynamics which emerge out of them. Failing that, we lose all chance to understand a part of our existence which, whether we like it or not, engages us and has a profound impact on how we perceive ourselves and our world and on how we live. Liken it to having a conversation with someone who is talking on the phone at the same time. At best it becomes difficult for the person engaged in the two conversations to keep them separate and to know to whom he's responding. As the conversations become more serious, separating them becomes more difficult. But it becomes infinitely more complex if neither you nor the person on the other end of the line knows that two conversations are going on simultaneously. Not only will he become hopelessly confused, so will you.

This is what happens when we engage our inner speakers during a conversation with another person. This is what was happening with Dana. Once she discovered what she was doing, she was in a better position to do something about it; like hanging up the phone and carrying on only one conversation at a time, to continue the analogy. Since we all carry within us our own psychological Trojan horses (Internal Witches or Demons) that emerge out of our childhood processes, we do carry on conversations with them from time to time to varying degrees of intensity. If we fail to recognize when we're engaged in a conversation with these Inner Others, our lives can become hopelessly confused. Once we begin to understand and acknowledge them, then we can take the steps to let go. This book will study the internal conversation and, more specifically, show how two people learned how to recognize it and let go of it.

Taking Charge

An important step in this task of recognition and letting go is the realization of a simple but difficult truth: the Inner Other is not a part of the "I." I have touched on this point earlier when dealing with the language shift from "I" to "you," but the separateness of the Inner Other and the "I" cannot be stressed too often. I frequently use a metaphor in helping people understand how the Inner Other is separate and operates autonomously from the "I": when Michelangelo, the artist, created the statue *David,* he drew his inspiration for that statue from another person, the model. The model was not *David,* and *David* was not the model. Likewise, the statue was not Michelangelo, nor Michelangelo the statue. Each maintained its own existence and existed independently of each other although there was a connection between them through causality and interaction.

Likewise, when we are children, we used our parents, siblings, and other members of the household as models from which we molded our Inner Others. Like the statue, these internal persons were not then nor are they now the historical persons of father, mother, sister, brother, nanny, or whomever, or the present-day persons either. They exist separately and independently of each other. Further, just as Michelangelo was not *David,* so too we are not our Inner Others nor are our Inner Others ourselves. We also exist separately and independently of each other.

That is not to say that there isn't an intimate connection and interaction between the two. Although they have separate existences, the energy by which the Inner Other operates in relationship to the "I" emerges from the "I" itself. If the "I" does not give it the energy to engage, then it cannot act; it simply becomes immobile and dormant. However, it is not destroyed. We only remove its power to interact with and engage us for a while. Just as Mary used words to disown her spontaneity and construct her Internal Mother and just as Dana used words to keep alive her Inner Other, the words we use determine whether we keep these images alive and in power or impotent and manageable. By listening carefully to what we say and how we say it, we can become conscious of the unconscious "keys" in the interaction between Inner Other and the "I." Once we become conscious of the "keys" we can begin to change the *de facto* dialogue that goes on between us and our Inner Other, and we can render it impotent, inactive, and non-functional. The power to create the Inner Other, the intruding force, had been Dana's just as it was ours. Likewise, the power to remove and eliminate this force forever was Dana's as it is ours. By understanding and correcting the misconceptions perpetrated by it, Dana would be able to claim and allow her own spontaneous, autonomous, valuable Self to emerge.

The Child-Within

Dana's first step on the road to psychological autonomy and an enriched sense of Self came out of her ability to acknowledge the presence of an inner speaker and to recognize certain patterns that enabled her to identify this voice as that of her Inner Other. It was this Inner Other who thwarted her self-directedness. In referring back to Dana's interchanges which have been noted here, there is another facet of this psychic process which emerges. From the depths of Dana's psyche emerges still another speaker which seems to have developed internally in relation to the dictates of Dana's Inner Other. Recall, when Dana asks herself, "Can I get up yet?" and replies "No, I can't get up yet, but I'm going to get up in fifteen minutes," her tone is pleading and the phrase, modifying. Even though this may lead us to believe that Dana was interacting with an internal authority, there isn't the pronoun shift which signals the presence of the Inner Other. In this case, both the question and the answer are framed in the first person. An answer to Dana's question along the line of "No, you can't get up yet, but you *will* get up in fifteen minutes," would lead us to recognize immediately the voice of the Inner Other. But this is not the case. Dana's use of "I" here seems to indicate that Dana was addressing not a separate antagonistic authority but an entity that appeared to be an integral part of Dana's true Self. In fact, Dana does describe this as a part of herself—weak but rebellious.

Along with the shift of pronouns, one of the basic clues signaling the presence of the inner speaker is a change in tone. From earlier examples, it's obvious that, along with the pronoun change, the tone changes as well and the response is usually demeaning and judgmental. In this case, while there is no shift in pronoun, there is a definite shift in tone. Moreover, far from being demeaning and judgmental, the tone of the response is passive and childlike. Dana's use of "I" in both the question and the response tells us that we are hearing the voice of a facet of Dana's true Self. However, the shift in tone seems to indicate that the speaker has an existence which is separate and distinct from Dana as an adult.

Part of the Self and yet separate from it: this idea is the paradox at the crux of Dana's psychic world. Again I recall Mary and Jane that afternoon in my apartment and how Jane's overbearing concern forced Mary to drive her childlike behavior and her childlike view of herself and her world far into the recesses of her psyche. I recall how later on Mary "punished" her doll for acting too childishly. Mary's mind seemed to discern a variety of messages from her mother's behavior, including the message that childlike spontaneity was unacceptable, so Mary disowned her own spontaneity to conform to her mother's demands. At the same time, Mary internalized these demands and incorporated them into the "personality" of her own evolving Inner Other which would act as an independent monitor curtailing Mary's spontaneity even when Jane was not present. However, the spontaneity does not disappear. Instead it's relocated—that was apparent that afternoon. Mary's spontaneity was projected onto her doll and Mary's developing Inner Other promptly punished the doll for such "naughty" behavior. In that act Mary, siding with her Internal Mother, disowned her own sense of Self contained within her spontaneity to accommodate the demands of the Internal

Mother. The projection of the spontaneity shows that it did not vanish. Rather, at this point in Mary's psychic development this behavior and all behavior of its kind became dissociated from the "I" (Mary's self-image) and was supplanted by the will of the Inner Other.

In Dana's case the dissociated parts of the "I"—those parts of her Self which she disowned as a child in the face of the demands and threats of her Inner Other—became the basis of another psychic entity which was pushed off into the realm of Dana's unconscious. This was Dana's Internal Child; here could be found the needs, desires, wishes, feelings, thoughts of a little girl, Dana. For a variety of reasons all of these facets of this little girl were shoved into limbo by the Inner Other but, while Dana had to separate herself from these "unacceptable" features of her personality, there's no doubt that these features came from the core of Dana's true Self. Embodied in Dana's Internal Child are these aspects which are undeniably Dana, but the pressure exerted on Dana to disown these various parts of herself finally caused a breach. That's why Dana's Internal Child, albeit a part of her true Self, remains separate and distinct from Dana now. Therefore, in a very real way this disowned part of the Self is a part of Dana's "I," but it does not function as a part of Dana's overall life flow. Dana's disowned child "I" emerged that morning after long periods of apparent dormancy. There was no doubt, however, that its continued emergence became the propelling force behind Dana's confusion, depression and anxiety and, finally, her need for therapy.

As long as the dictates of Dana's Inner Other were operative, Dana functioned like an automaton without needs or feelings. For long periods at a time the Inner Other guidance system "worked," and Dana lived out her life in inertia. But there were times when the system broke down and, during these periods, its prime objective of suppressing the Inner Child simply malfunctioned. It was during these periods that Dana's child "I" emerged and, in the face of renewed demands, behaved like a child—weak, vulnerable, somewhat helpless, but not without a strategy towards its fight for survival. On occasion it would plead but more often it rebelled. In Dana's case the forms of resistance used by her Inner Child against the demands of her

Inner Other were obvious: passive resistance. ("No, I can't get up yet, but I'm going to get up in fifteen minutes"); obstinacy ("I'd rather continue to lie there than write those letters"); and pleading ("I can't!").

Unfortunately, these forms of resistance were weak in comparison to the demands of the Inner Other which, like a real parent in the eyes of a child, remained the center of Dana's internal world and had to remain there at all costs. But the Inner Child remained very much alive and active. Dana's life had become a "draw" between these two important forces in which, from time to time, for one reason or another, there would be a momentary shift in power to one side or the other. The shift generated enormous anxiety which then motivated her desperately to try to bring back the original balance of power which was only a standoff that was nothing less than physical and psychological immobility. Whenever she tried to shift out of the immobility, the standoff was upset and she was in the midst of the anxiety again. The only real option that was open to her was to reevaluate the nature of the internal balance of power she assumed she had to maintain in order to feel comfortable about her life.

All of this raises a further and much deeper question: "Who is the Dana who found herself sandwiched between the person of the Inner Other and the dissociated person of the 'Child-I'?"

The Central "I"

It is clear that there is a third participant in this psychic tug of war.

Earlier, when Dana recalled the events of that morning, we were able to recognize the dissociated child "I" with whom she engaged in an overt but brief conversation in the exchange "Can I get up yet? . . . No, I can't get up yet, but I'm going to get up in fifteen minutes." We have clearly identified the child "I" answering the question but who is asking it?

This same question must be raised when Dana alternated between knowing and not knowing what she wanted to do that morning. At one point a seemingly self-directed Dana was able to identify what she wanted to do: to putter with her hands. That quickly dissolved into the self-doubt: " . . . The trouble is that on days like this I don't seem to know what my true desires and needs are. I don't *know* what I want to do." Again, who is it who is bounced back and forth between knowing and not knowing?

There is a part of Dana that was trapped in the battle between the Inner Other voice and the dissociated "Child-I." That part moved in whatever direction either one of the other two combatants who was in power at the moment pushed it. The point is, there was an "it" that was being pushed around by the other two personae. This third part I have come to call the Central "I."

When a person like Dana possesses a very powerful Inner Other, the Self, the "I," is split into two parts with the Inner Other acting as a wedge between them. These two parts are the "Child-I" and the Central "I." The "Child-I" exists mainly in the dark realm of the unconscious only to emerge momentarily and sometimes eruptively as it did that morning in reaction to the overbearing activity of the powerful, intrusive Inner Other.

The Central "I," on the other hand, is the part of the Self that exists, as it were, with one foot in the internal unconscious realm and the other in the conscious reality of the Self in relation to the world of outside persons and events. In a very real way the Central "I" acts as a bridge between what is happening within the internal reality comprised of the interaction between the Inner Other and the "Child-I" and external reality—Dana's interaction with other persons like her husband or me. It was Dana as the Central "I" who was most apparent to the onlooker. It was this part of Dana that acted as the negotiator, arbitrator, or mediator in all the arguments that erupted between the Inner Other and the "Child-I." As we saw in the very brief transcript, this battle between these internal fighters not only disturbed Dana internally but sent shock waves through Dana's existence in her external world as well. In this particular case, her ability to do things, to putter with her plants, walk the dog, write letters was severely compromised. This same battle radically altered how Dana related to people, her husband, friends, business associates, and even me. It was the Central "I" of Dana that negotiated this very complex task. The negotiations that Dana as Central "I" had entered into up to this point in her life had been ruled by some very erroneous and rigid beliefs about herself, the "Child-I," and the Inner Other.

Part II

THE CONFLICT

3

COMING TO SELF-AWARENESS

"I" Identity

The "I" of any human person is a rather complex psychological reality. Dana's "I" had been split into parts. Regardless of that, however, these "parts" had qualities that, although they were now disparate, were never destroyed. To understand better what these intrinsic qualities of the "I" are, whether as a unified or divided "I," I would like to share an early but very important personal childhood experience I once had.

Early one spring in New York City, from where I sat in my office, I could see the sun weaving a golden thread through the milky clouds above the Palisades across the Hudson. Dana's session had just ended and, since I had some time before my next appointment, I sat listening to the tape of our conversation. One question in particular stuck in my mind. I'd asked her to describe her earliest childhood memory and now as I heard myself ask that question on the tape, my mind plunged into my own shadowed memories. The images sped by as recollections of earlier events took hold and grew. Suddenly I had a picture in my mind and I knew by intuition or by instinct that it represented a crucial moment in my life. At first the imagery was separate but soon I was able to piece it all together. . . .

It was Easter Sunday and I was sitting on the back steps of our house. I was three or four at the time and I was thoroughly enjoying a warm spring day. In fact, it was warmer than usual. I remember how blue the sky was that day—it was like a robin's egg—and how the clouds like white smoke from a fantastic earth-fire along the horizon seemed to transform that sky into a backdrop for scenes from a fairy tale. The clouds were giants and then fantastic animals; towering castles and beautiful ladies; it was all there. My mind wandered and I lost all sense of time. The drone of a passing plane had a hypnotic effect and, in a sleepy rhythm, wound its way around the continuous hum of a swarm of bees in the distance—a musical counterpoint to the scenes in my mind's eye. I turned my head and caught a glimpse of the sun. It was pale gold—almost silver—but it gleamed magnificently and I saw its beams jut through the clouds and across the universe. I had to squint and just at that moment I noticed a curious thing: from between my eyes there was this protusion. Amazing! And I hadn't noticed it before. At first I stared at it and then I double-checked it with my hands. Of course, it was my nose; I'd seen that in the mirror many times before—but this was different. I was seeing my nose from a very special perspective—I was seeing my nose as only I could see it!!! And then I realized an incredible fact: I and only I of all the people in the world—no, in the universe—could see my nose in this way. I was looking out of these little windows and they were reserved for me only. They were my windows—my eyes. No one else could see out of my windows or see my nose just like I did.

Unlike all of my previous experiences as a child, this became crucial because it provided me with a sense of my own uniqueness. I realized for the first time in my existence that I was the only person in the world who could do this—peer at the world from inside me! And, of course, that I was the only me!

Along with this realization came an awareness of my separateness from others.

"I Am" Separateness

In that moment of clarity, a number of insights seeded themselves within me that would continue to grow and have a profound impact on me and how I viewed the world about me. The first insight I had at that moment was, **I AM.** For the first time in my life I was aware that I was aware of myself. I am who I am. I am an "I."

Beyond that initial insight of my awareness another followed quickly upon it; not only was I aware of myself but I was now aware that *I* was completely unique in that newfound awareness. Not only did I discover that I am who I am but I also discovered my radical separateness from others. I possessed an inner existence within the parameters of my body and that existence was mine alone. But further, within those parameters my identity was inviolable. While forces outside of myself might lead me to act in such a manner as to betray my inner integrity or while others might cajole, manipulate, or force me in such a way that I'd appear to be someone other than myself, no one would totally obliterate that inner existence. Emanating from within me came my sense of who I am and despite the onslaughts from without, that sense of "I" could remain intact. No matter how hard someone would tell me what I was or should be wanting, needing, thinking, knowing, or feeling, I could always maintain the "I" integrity and identity from within, no matter to what lengths I had to go to change the outward appearances.

As I have grown older, wiser, and more articulate, the event of that Easter Sunday has taught me another reality about my self-awareness. This early experience of self-awareness is tied inextricably to my senses and thoughts. My body's ability to feel, see, smell, and finally to reflect on those sensations comprises what I call "stimulation states." But I must point out that I was not only feeling but I was also thinking. "This is *my* nose! *I* am!" In the stimulation of the feeling and the thinking, I became aware of "I am." It is when I actively receive, integrate, engage in, and respond to these stimulation states that I become aware that I am. The stimulation states, therefore, are not self-awareness itself but lead to it. Somehow through the process of being stimulated, I become self-aware. In addition to all of these realizations about my "I," there is one more quality about it I've come to realize.

Self-awareness is also timeless. Not only am I aware that I am, but I am aware that I am *without change* in time as well. That "I" which became self-aware so many years ago sitting on those steps is the very same "I" who sits here reflecting at this moment. Yes, changes have occurred: some of my opinions have changed; my knowledge has grown; my sensations and perceptions of the world have altered from moment to moment, but the central awareness of myself has remained unaltered, unchanged and everpresent. **I AM WHO I AM** and no event in time ever changes or alters that single truth.

This observation about a reality of my psychological existence is confirmed to be a universal experience when we look at some of the experimental data that are at our disposal. During the 1960s psychologists began to investigate the experiences of various subjects under sensory deprivation. In these experiments, the subjects were placed in environments that were devoid of the most usual means of sensory stimulation: specially designed tanks which minimized the awareness of their own bodies. This was done to prevent the normal, subtle bodily (kinesthetic) sensations that we take for granted from being a part of the subject's experience. Then they were blindfolded and placed in a water-filled capsule which was soundproofed, maintained at body temperature and a constant zero-gravity level. Like the experiment simulated in the motion picture "Altered States," the subjects soon fell into a deep sleep. When they awoke, they spent most of the time making attempts at autostimulation, usually by talking to themselves or moving around. Without success they'd lapse back into long periods of deep sleep. Gradually, the periods of awakened awareness became more frequent and the sleep spans grew shorter. The subjects' behavior became notably restless and their attempts at autostimulation more pronounced and, at times, frantic. Their talking rapidly faded into gibberish. Eventually, they began to hear voices answering them and carried on what seemed to be a two-way conversation. They experienced auditory and visual hallucinations, which they could no longer separate from reality. When the subjects later related what they'd experienced at this last stage of the experiment, they all reported a terrible panic tied into their loss of a sense of who they were. It was as if they could no longer separate the outside world from their inner realities and, after making attempts to hold onto themselves in vain, they panicked.

Obviously, outside stimulus is crucial in the maintenance of our own sense of "I." The subjects in this experiment were cut off from such outside stimuli to an extreme and, so to speak, the auditory and visual hallucinations were produced to compensate for this detrimental lack of external stimuli. Acting as a monitor, the mind cued in on this deprivation and projected some kind of sensory experience in an attempt to adjust to the extreme environment and allow the individual to maintain a sense of "I" in spite of it. Unfortunately, the mind's projections were completely unconnected to reality; so, while they allowed the subject to maintain a sense of "I," the subject "experienced" a wholly internal and unreal world. As awareness of Self fails in proportion to the absence of outside stimuli, the "I" panics. It is confronted with its own dissolution—psychological death—and at this juncture internal projections or hallucinations take over.

All human beings in that "heart of darkness" understand the delicate balance between sensation and self-awareness. Just as I at that early age became conscious of myself as a separate, unique, and self-aware creature through the stimulation of my environment, so it must be with all of us. Obviously, for most people this is not something appreciated on an intellectual level, but it's something that is understood nonetheless. As self-aware beings we must maintain certain levels of stimulation, and their importance to the survival of the "I" compels us to preserve the sources of stimulation at our disposal. There are two sources of all stimulation: internal—internal thoughts, mental images and kinesthetics; and external—interaction with the external environment of both animate and inanimate objects. If we are in danger of losing either source of stimulation, we will work intensely, using all means at our disposal, to prevent the loss, or make every attempt to restore it, or fall back on remaining sources of stimulation by heightening them. In cases where there is a severe loss of stimulation (as in the experiment described earlier) the "I" compensates for the loss by providing stimulation from within itself, creating imaginary persons and objects with which it can interact to maintain a minimal level of stimulation. It is thus able to stay alive psychologically.

Because she had been so successful at disconnecting from herself, Dana also lost her ability to claim her own stimulation states. This resulted in her experiencing herself as disappearing or dying psychologically. When that happened, she became anxious. At these times, her "Child-I" was activated to claim back momentarily the needed sense of identity through the stimulation states. When it seemed that the Inner Other was taking everything away, psychological death became too imminent and the Child stepped in to claim *something*, even if only in rebelling. The act of rebellion on the part of Dana's "Child-I" was motivated by her as an *act of survival* in a very real sense for the entire "I" identity of Dana. The "Child-I" of Dana, however, had cut off communication with her and listened only to the Inner Other who told her two things, both of which were lies. The first was that this part of her was dangerous and her death would result if she listened to the "Child-I." Secondly, the Inner Other told her it was the source of life because if she listened to it, she would do everything "right," everyone would like her, and because of that she would gain life through their approval.

Because the Central "I" of Dana made this kind of allegiance and because she was "in charge" most of the time, she often made death types of choices. When this happened and Dana as a Self was very much in danger, the "Child-I" would temporarily break out of her internal prison and for a moment, as she did that morning, pull both of them away from that terrible peril of total loss of "I" identity.

The Other as Affirmation of "I"

Of all external stimulation the most powerful and intense comes from our interaction with other human beings. Since external stimulation is crucial to the affirmation and preservation of the "I," it follows that human beings who have been deprived of the stimulating interaction with adult figures in their early lives should bear the results of this deprivation in behavior patterns as adolescents and even later on as adults. Experiments with infant monkeys indicated a notably higher infant mortality for those animals deprived of the dynamic interaction with mothering monkeys than those who had known the stimulation of their mother's proximity. Also, for those monkeys who survived, the deprived monkeys could be singled out for their irritability, withdrawal from interaction with other monkeys, inactivity, poor appetite, and a severely limited or nonexistent sex life.

Studies of this kind have shown over and over again that deprivation of the stimulation afforded by the parenting figure during the developmental stages of life causes the adult mammal to lose the ability to cope successfully with its environment and, most drastically, to lose the power to interact with and reproduce those of its own kind. The mammal who suffers this kind of deprivation is restricted in its ability to maintain its integrity as an organism because it is maladapted in managing its environment to sustain its own life. It is too timid to move about or seek a wider spectrum of stimuli in an attempt to preserve itself. Such an organism perceives itself primarily as being attacked by its own environment; consequently it is oriented towards its defense *against* its environment rather than towards its growth *through* the environment.

When we add the dimension of self-awareness that is possessed by humans, the importance of the stimulation that is received in the social interaction and the possibility of its being lost through faulty interactions with others during the social and psychological developmental years can be overwhelming to the human subject.

Without a doubt, the psychological threat to the integrity of the "I" is woven into the fabric of our culture. The worst punishment that society has imposed on individuals or groups for a variety of reasons has been to ostracize them from the mainstream of human experience and hence deprive them of the stimulation we reap from interaction with others. Certainly the most severe cases in point are solitary confinement or exile. In the first case the person's crime is deemed so heinous that he is deprived of all human contact for a period of time. Certainly, this is an extreme situation, but how much more prevalent in our society are individuals exiled or cut off from the mainstream. While we usually associate exile with primitive tribes who banished an offender, or with high-ranking politicians (or with the nobility of ages past) who are deposed and exiled, our society offers many more immediate examples of exile. One has only to think of the way minority groups have been treated in modern times to understand the effects of exile. The Jews of Europe not too long ago experienced the effects of exile by being forced to live in ghettos and concentration camps; the Blacks in many modern states, including our own, still endure the deprivation of exile by being socially and economically and, in many cases, geographically outcast; homosexuals in many countries are only now coming to grips with the effect banishment has had on them as a group and as individuals. In certain totalitarian states separation is essential to the "social reorientation" (brainwashing) of its dissident citizens. All of these cases of separation from the mainstream of society play on the human fear of death, a fear which entails a great deal more than the dread of the unknown or biological dissolution. It represents the radical and eternal separation from others and, at its most frightening core, the utter dissolution of Self. Often the conscious or unconscious purpose behind government or culture treating an individual or group in this way is to render them powerless by removing from the very "stuff" of life the will to live. If one's awareness of Self is low because it does not have the stimulation that emerges out of social interaction, then the energy that can be invested in living is not there, because the basic necessity for an awareness of psychological life is either absent or radically diminished by loss of contact with important others or with a familiar environment.

We need not limit solitary confinement or banishment to large impersonal governmental or cultural structures. This same principle can and often is used at the immediate, personal family level. It is often exercised against family members who do not conform to the norms and agendas set up by other (often more powerful) family members. The threat of real or psychological banishment from the hub of the family can be quite enough to keep most (usually less powerful, that is, children) family members conforming and in line.

In fact, the human drive to maintain the "I" is affirmed to such a degree that our fear of physical death can become a secondary consideration. Obviously, when considering two extraordinarily powerful fears, it's difficult to judge which one maintains the greater force, but while there is no doubt that we understand the tremendous motivation behind self-preservation and the fear of death, by comparison we understand very little about the equally powerful motivation behind the fear of psychological death of dissolution of the "I." Throughout the pages of history there have been stories of people who preferred death over the dissolution of their sense of Self. Those who opt for this we label as martyrs. It's not that the fear of death doesn't motivate such individuals: it motivates us all. But what most of these individuals have in common is an acute sense of Self which makes even the notion of the dissolution of the "I" far more abhorrent than biological dissolution.

In human development a child's sense of closeness to a mothering figure is essential for healthy growth and maturation, but equally important to the quantity of holding and feeding is the quality of that contact. Infants who experience their mothering figures as tense or indifferent but are held regularly develop the same problems as infants who are only infrequently held: later they mature into adults who exhibit the same neurotic symptoms observed in the behavior of the research monkeys discussed earlier. When compared to infants who experienced a high quality and quantity of holding and feeding, these other infants show a high susceptibility to physical illnesses like colic and bacterial and viral infections. In fact, Dana's reporting that she herself was prone to infections and abdominal disorders at an unusually high rate gave me the first clue to a missed closeness with a mothering figure during her infancy.

Around 18 months the child has already completed the process of "imprinting." At this point in the child's internal life its mothering figure has been psychically entrenched as an irreplaceable object upon whom it is wholly dependent for contact with its external world and for stimulation given to the child by this person. Mothers and babysitters are especially familiar with the effects of "imprinting," but anyone who knows or has known a child of this age should be able to recall such an example as the one which follows:

> The weather is cool and windy today, so Joan decides that she won't take the baby Judy along to the doctor. Her appointment is at 3:30 and the regular babysitter gets out of school at 3:00—she hopes she's not too late. She's waiting by the door for the babysitter to arrive. The baby is playing with her toys on the living room floor. Joan hopes that Judy is occupied enough so that she can leave without being noticed. The babysitter arrives and mother is about to disappear down the hall when she hears a blood-curdling scream: obviously, baby has something to say (!!!) about mother's departure.

Most of us can relate this to our own experiences as children or with other children. What we probably don't readily appreciate is that, once the baby realizes that its mother is absent, nothing short of its mother's return will alter the child's discomfort at the mother's absence. The child simply cannot reason that mother will return, and it responds, even to a brief departure of its mother, as to a life-threatening experience. The child knows from past experiences that clinging and crying tend to summon its mother and keep her by its side, so, to appease the anxiety caused by this separation, this is exactly what the child is determined to do.

Crying and clinging help the child remedy a physical separation from its mother, but to combat still another form of parent/child separation, the child uses a more complex and subtle system of reckoning with its loss. When the child is the object of parental disfavor, it experiences psychological and emotional loss of the parent. That is to say, the loss of parental favor constitutes emotional and psychological abandonment with its concomitant death threat. The child recognizes the overwhelming force that such a loss exerts on its psychological life and makes the necessary psychological adjustments to thwart this kind of response from its parent(s). The steps are the beginnings of still another process in the psychological life of the child. Around the age of three the child becomes psychologically capable of forming internalized images of the approving and disapproving external parent. It is in response to the possibility of parental disfavor or rejection that the child erects an image of the parent in its psyche and centers this image in its internal world. The thrust of the internal image is two-fold: (1) It provides the child with a value system based on its earlier interactions with its parent and, in such a way, can become a monitor by which the child can scrutinize internally all possible avenues of action. If the child plays with matches or dashes out into the middle of the street, the monitor will signal parental disfavor. The child's motivation for heeding the monitor's signal is the promise of a loving and approving response from its real parent. (2) It allows the child to maintain at least a mental relationship with a parent which the child perceives it has lost or will lose through an act of disobedience.

When properly motivated, this process is fundamental to the development of the child's sense of right and wrong and its selection of appropriate behavior in relation to itself and others.

As the child grows older, this process enables it to see for itself the danger in running out into the middle of the street or the violation of another's rights in interrupting while someone else is speaking. The child begins to understand for itself the inappropriateness of such spontaneous action. The demands of the real parent and, therefore, the demands of the internal image have a consistency and logic which the child can appreciate and understand. It's important that the parent convey to the child the sense that the child's behavior or emotional state be altered because there is some intrinsic reason for the change which the parent recognizes and the child is also to understand. If this doesn't occur, then the child perceives that it must alter its behavior simply because its parent says so and that it is not capable of using its own resources to monitor and judge its own behavior. The ultimate message the child receives is that its parent is the sole and ultimate authority, and this authority cannot be questioned, reasoned with, or even understood! Unfortunately, the child who receives such a parental message constructs a mental image in kind: an image that must be consulted before any action; an image whose dictates are beyond the child's reason and comprehension. In such a position, the "I" is perpetually perplexed and anxious about the kind of reactions it gets from this seemingly irreplaceable judge.

To understand this process in the parent/child relationship, it's important to see just how it manifests itself in the everyday relating between parent and child. In the child's formative years, the parent's role as the child's life-task teacher is crucial in preparing the child for its life outside the family unit, and it's out of this context that some of the best examples come to mind. The interaction between parent and child when the parent teaches the child something as basic as how to tie its own shoelaces can offer us some insight into the kind of parenting the child undergoes and, as a result, the kind of mental image it constructs.

Not only the words the parent uses in its interaction with the child but also the way the parent approaches and interacts with the child and the parent's verbal and attitudinal tone are important in giving or not giving the child a strong sense of Self.

Lesson A

Cast

Deborah is the mother of five-year-old Mary who has just started first grade. It's evening; Mary is playing in the living room while Deborah sits nearby reading a magazine. The interaction begins like this:

Mary: Mommy, teach me how to tie my shoelaces, please.
Deborah: Sure Mary. Say, I have some time now. Would you like to learn now?
Mary: Yes, Mommy, yes!
Deborah: Okay, Mary, tell you what. You come over here and I'll sit beside you and you watch what I do, okay?

[Deborah then slowly proceeds to tie the shoelaces on Mary's shoes, trying to break the tying process down into discrete steps. When she is finished she asks Mary:]

Would you like to try now?
Mary: Yes [excitedly].

[Mary then begins. Being unused to the task she is clumsy and awkward. She frequently fumbles and makes mistakes.]

Deborah: Looks like you're having a problem there.
Mary: Yes. Can you help me, Mommy?
Deborah: Okay—See what I do when I get to this point. Okay, I'm going to do it again. This time I'm going to tie my shoelace while you are doing yours, okay?
Mary: Yes.

[Deborah and Mary work together until Mary is successful at tying her shoelace. It's not the perfect bow and Mary is still awkward, unsure and cumbersome with the process. When Mary completes her first bow Deborah says:]

Deborah: Hey! That's good! See, you can do it! Now I'll bet if you practice that, you'll be able to tie your own shoelaces by yourself in a couple of days! What do you think?
Mary: [With excitement and joy] Yeah, that was fun, Mommy. I can't wait to show Daddy. Can we do it once more, Mommy?
Deborah: Sure. I'm going to have to start supper soon, but I can help you once more. I'll bet you'll be able to work on your own while I'm busy, though. So let's try again.

Lesson B

Cast

In another setting, six-year-old Dana is getting ready for school. Janet, her mother, is helping.

> Janet: Dana [with some irritation in her voice] when are you going to learn how to dress yourself? I think it's time you learned to tie your shoelaces. Come on over here, we haven't got much time! [Dana comes over and stands facing Janet.] You watch me and then I want you to try. [Janet ties the shoes the way she would tie them any other time, except she does it a little more slowly than she normally does. When she's finished she says:] Okay, Dana, now you do it.

[Dana is feeling somewhat anxious and confused but begins to fumble at tying. When she is unsuccessful, Janet says to her impatiently]:

> No, you can't do it that way! Can't you learn anything? Watch!

[Again she impatiently ties the shoelace. Again she commands Dana to do it. Dana begins again, this time close to tears. She fumbles again and Janet begins to shout]

> God, are *you* stupid! You can't learn anything. Now we're late for school. Give me your foot and I'll tie them! It just seems as though you can't do anything right! I guess I'm going to have to do everything for you. Come on, let's go!

Obviously, there is a vast difference between the way Deborah and Janet relate to their children. What the child creates as its Inner Other is dependent on the way in which the parental figure relates. Therefore the differing messages Deborah and Janet communicate are important if we are to understand the dynamics of the internal voices.

The scene itself communicates a profound difference between the ways Deborah and Janet relate to their children. For Mary the task of learning to tie her shoelaces begins in a neutral atmosphere in which both mother and child are quietly with each other. This is not so between Dana and her mother. The scene is not neutral. There are other tasks that need to be completed and must be completed within a fairly rigid framework (getting to school on time). Therefore, the circumstances of learning a fairly complex motor task certainly could not be described as being neutral.

There is a radical difference regarding initiative. In lesson A, Mary, the child, takes the initiative which implies at some level that she sees it as important that *she* learn how to tie her shoelaces. In lesson B, the initiative is taken by the parent and again there is a mixed agenda: Does Janet want to teach Dana how to tie her shoelaces, or is Janet irritated by the task (and maybe the morning rush) and looking for a scapegoat for her irritation?

Deborah maintains the unthreatening emotional atmosphere in response to Mary by examining her own time boundaries and finds that she in fact has the time to *freely* respond to Mary's request and undertake the task. This is not so for Janet. The interaction begins in a tension that continues to build. It is heightened by her remark, "We haven't got much time."

The way the parents physically position themselves tells us more about how they relate to their children and the messages they communicate to them. Deborah positions herself in such a way that the viewpoint from which the child watches her perform the task is the same as the viewpoint the child will have when she performs the task herself. Janet does not do this. She positions herself in such a way that the child must switch everything around—a relatively involved task for anyone, let alone a child.

Deborah further lessens the complexity of the task by breaking it down into simple, discrete steps. Janet, however, does not empathize at all with the complexity of the task as it appears to the child. She approaches the child as if this were not a new learning task at all. In fact, she approaches the shoe-tying lesson as though it were just another event in *her* day and not a new event for Dana.

Because Deborah has been aware that the child is learning a new and complicated motor task she has tried to accommodate herself to Mary's position. Mary can now see that the task, her task, is within her grasp. Dana, on the other hand, is in a very different position. Her mother has not recognized the complexity or the newness of the task and has approached Dana as though she is a little adult who should have some innate capability to perform the task. Dana, therefore, approaches the task as one that defies her comprehension as well as being a task that is not even her own.

As Mary and Dana approach their task, there is a qualitative difference in the way both are responded to. Deborah responds to Mary's mistakes and fumbling with reassuring words and tone as well as with participatory problem solving (both she and Mary solve the problem). But even prior to that, because of the warm atmosphere, Mary sees herself as being able to turn to her mother as a resource. Not so with Janet. She responds to Dana's learning situation as though her fumbling is an insult, and she attacks Dana's capabilities when she says: "Can't you learn anything?" This is an attack on Dana's value as a person. "God, are *you* stupid!" The *pièce de résistance* comes when she then blames Dana for being the cause of the lateness rather than admit that she chose an unrealistic time to teach her daughter a task like this.

The results of the interactions place Mary and Dana in two completely different realms of relationship. Mary completes her task. Deborah accepts it for what it is, the first bow tied by a little girl, a major motor accomplishment. Because it was complicated and it was the first time, it was not *the* perfect bow. But Deborah rejoices with Mary in her accomplishment and encourages her to improve so that Mary can become increasingly independent of the dependent child/parent relationship.

Dana, however, is not so lucky. She does not complete her task. She fails not because of her own inadequacy but because of the inadequacy and inappropriate parenting of her mother. The irony is that her mother pins the failure of the activity on her. Having done that, she then tells Dana she cannot survive in the world without her mother to help her.

What kind of messages do these two children incorporate and then construct into the internalized object-persons?

Mary	*Dana*
1. She can set her own agenda as her needs become apparent to her. A	1. Somebody else sets up the agenda. The agenda is one in which she is not

Mary

task is usually free of conflict. The voice is not present because the subject is working out of its own center and is not dependent on some other as authority.

2. Tasks are usually unthreatening: they are perceived as "do-able" because they can be broken into "do-able" parts. The voice encourages and offers constructive suggestions as to how to solve the problem.

3. The Inner Other is a resource to whom the subject can turn with confidence. The voice not only encourages and offers instructive suggestions but also suggests to the subject that the real performer is the subject and the voice is only auxiliary.

4. As subject she can succeed—and mostly under her own power. The fundamental message of

Dana

even consulted. There is often a mixed agenda. As any agenda is approached, there is anxiety because any task is begun as an unpleasant burden—and she is to blame for the unpleasantness. Therefore the voice determines the agenda and blames the subject for the "unpleasantness" of the task even before the task is begun.

2. Tasks are usually threatening because they appear as incomprehensible in their complexity. The voice discourages as it says, "You can't do that because it's too complex." Any suggestion it may offer beyond that is destructive.

3. The Inner Other is one who criticizes and upholds unattainable standards of achievement. When those standards aren't met (of course), the subject becomes the object of a barrage of charges of incompetency, personal valuelessness, and guilt.

4. In addition to everything else that has been incorporated into the internal object-voice to

Mary

the voice to Mary is, "You can do it. I will help you along, but you've got the resources within you." In other words, because of the parenting model she had, Mary's voice has a self-destruct mechanism so that one day Mary will be able to say to herself, "Yes, *I* have the resources within me to take care of almost any task I may find before me. And if I don't I can find someone who can help me."

Dana

this point, the voice tells her, "You will not complete any task (so why start?). Your not completing the task is due to your incompetency, stupidity, and worthlessness as a person. And, finally, because you are incompetent, stupid, and worthless, you cannot survive without me. (I've proven that already.) So you had better not try."

Unlike Mary, Dana's internal object-voice does not have a self-destruct mechanism. Quite the contrary, it is in there to stay because it threatens the subject with annihilation if the subject should try to do anything on its own. Therefore, Dana and people like her go through life believing that their internal object-voice is their lifeline (umbilical cord) to survival, when actually it is the chain that entraps them in a living death.

A legitimate question might be asked at this point: "If the Inner Other proves to be such a problem in the later development of a person, what is its function and adaptive advantage in the psychological development of a human being?"

One of the primary ways the child becomes self-aware is through its experience of the Other as an Other. There comes a time in the development of the child when it "discovers" the word "no." During this period, which overlaps both with its fear of being abandoned by its parents and especially its mother and the creation of the internal parents, it seems as though every other word out of its mouth is "no"—even, at times, right after a child has said "no" to something, it turns around and does it or responds in affirmation.

Through the use of this verbal device the child is exploring how far its personal "territory" extends and where it ends. Part of practicing the "no" involves its up-against-ness in relation to the Other. "This is how far I can go before I come up against the Other." In a primitive way, the child is discovering who it is.

The Inner Other is a psychological mechanism by which this process of boundary-setting is achieved internally. As the child develops a capability to internalize the parental limits its sense of up-against-ness (this is where I end and you begin) is also intensified and internalized. Many would agree that without this process of internalization there cannot evolve a solid sense of "I" identity. The construction of the parental image is essential to the establishment of a solid sense of "I-ness" and is a very adaptive psychological mechanism. The fault in the system of the Inner Other for Dana and others like her is not in the programmed psychological mechanism; rather it is in the parental model which the child finds as *the* given in its developmental environment.

For Mary, the internalized message is one in which Mary's internal powers are adequate, of value, and respected by the Other. The Other is a reference for the Self and not a displacement of it. Because of this, the Inner Other is programmed through the message of the model to diminish in importance until it is supplanted by the subject's own ability to experience itself in its environment, assimilate that experience, and then come to judgments upon which it acts in relation to its environment. The subject "I" becomes its own reference point and ultimate authority. A self-destruct mechanism is built into the image of the Inner Other.

This is not true for Dana. Through the type of interaction of the example, the child is being taught that she does not have an existence that is her own. Any existence she does have is fundamentally connected to and dependent on the parenting figure. Dana can only do and be what the parental figure decides. If she does not conform to that external permission and instruction, she is attacked, belittled, and told she is responsible for any apparent dysfunction and failure. This is the inner propaganda she hears which, in her vulnerability, malleability, and incompleteness as an "I" identity, she incorporates as her Inner Other voice.

As she struggles to come to a realization of her "I" identity, she is confronted with new inner voices that combat her attempts to draw from her own resources and power. Because this now-internal voice blocks her from drawing on her resources and power, she cannot experience herself as having inner resources and power. Once that happens the sense of intrinsic Self that flows from that sense of power is radically altered. Rather than experiencing the "I" as substantial, full, valuable, worthy, and powerful, the "I" experiences itself as insubstantial, empty, valueless, worthless, and powerless.

But beyond *that* experience of itself it also hears from *within* the voice which screams at it: "You *are* insubstantial, empty, valueless, worthless, and powerless. The only way you can make up for that void is if you listen to me and fill up that void with the meaning and power I give you. If you don't do that and don't listen to me, you will have to fall back on your own void."

When hearing this kind of propaganda from within, the subject perceives itself as worthless and empty. The worthlessness and emptiness, in turn, rob the subject of power—it is immobilized. The subject then discovers in its inability to act a loss of confirmation of who it is, and so, the outside world confirms the propaganda that it is empty.

The fault, then, does not lie in this psychological mechanism. If there is continually appropriate parenting by Important Others in the child's environment, the mechanism will help bring the developing child to an awareness of its own autonomy, uniqueness, power, and identity. But if the relating to the child by Important Others is continually faulty, rather than bringing the developing child to a sense of identity, the resultant Inner Other will not only block that child in its most important of psychological tasks but it will, in addition, keep itself very much alive within the child with attacks and threats. Because the Inner Other remains so much alive from within, the subject can never seem to get beyond it to experience itself differently from what it is told from within. Rather than "self-destructing" in the way it is designed to do, this essential psychological mechanism becomes an endless "essentially necessary" tyrant. So intense and necessary can this inner tyrant be that the subject hears and experiences more of it in the inner reality that, although the subject believes it is experiencing external object-persons, it is not. Again, when it experiences outside others as attacking and threatening itself, it is afraid to become engaged with outside others. But because it retreats from outside Others, it unwittingly falls into a deeper and more dependent relationship with the Inner Other.

As a child, Dana, like other children, experienced the disapproval of her Important Others as a loss of their love. Because the sense of self-identity is so wrapped up in the Others' responses, the loss of love from the Important Others carries with it the loss of self-identity, i.e., self-awareness. The child's interpersonal options are psychologically and to a certain extent physically limited to the family environment. If the interpersonal options are in any way jeopardized, the stimulation derived from them is likewise endangered. The sense of self-awareness that comes from that stimulation is undermined. Therefore, with the familial disapproval, Dana was confronted with the threat of psychological death—the loss of self-awareness.

Another facet of the psychological function of the child's ability to internalize and image the Important Others is that it protects the child from the threat of being overwhelmed, or psychological death, which works in two ways.

(1) With the ability to internalize warnings, prohibitions, threats, and punishments, the child is in a better position to avoid the activity the Important Other prohibits. If the child can avoid them, obviously it can better avoid the disapproval and punishment of that figure and everything that follows upon that.

(2) Once the internalized image is established, an intense psychic relationship is established with that personal, internalized object. Therefore, even though the child may experience

a loss of the external Important Other, the child is able to maintain a relationship with its internal Important Other. This, in turn, can be done in either of two ways. The first way is to act out what the Important Other approves of and then to play out in the words of that other the approval that would be derived from that action. For example, although the child has already met with Mommy's disapproval, scolding and spanking for having taken the pots and pans out of the cabinet, the child goes to the dollhouse and puts everything back in order. It then plays out Mother's approval by saying to a doll: "What a good girl you are for taking care of the house so well." Not only does the child vicariously regain some of the approval but it also keeps the personal object relationship very much alive through the imaging. In so doing it keeps the stimulation of the interpersonal event alive and its sense of self-awareness as well. The second way is for the child to play out the scenario in a disobedient way. This time, the dollhouse is left a shambles. Mother's voice is not of approval, but of disapproval. "You naughty girl! Shame on you for leaving the house that way!" Although the internalized relationship has a decidedly negative flavor, it is a relationship and a very intense one at that, with the intensity residing in the guilt, anger, and hurt of the event. Mother's presence is very much there for the child through the mother image and the interaction with it.

This was the means by which Dana kept alive her tenuous relationships with her Important Others. Although these internalized figures continued to impose restrictions on her need for self-expression, she clung to these images in order to preserve her need for interpersonal contact and stimulation which, in turn, fed her sense of self-awareness through that mode of stimulation.

But, as we saw earlier, these internalized images really robbed her of her self-identity. Because of her reference as a developing identity, she believed something about them that was not true—that they were the source of her life and identity. Because of that misbelief she nurtured them inside herself and gave more and more of her personal power over to them. The more she did that, the more she needed them, so that by the time she reached chronological adulthood, the internalized Others were extremely powerful and Dana's identity was derived mainly from them; Dana's own identity was very cloudy to herself and to the persons around her. This self-doubt and confusion were apparent to her and those around her.

In addition to this process of internalization there was the simultaneous dissociation from aspects of herself which Dana perceived as unacceptable to the Important Others. These unclaimed and disclaimed parts of her "I" became a separate entity within the Self. We have already identified this psychic entity as the Inner Child. It is now apparent why "Child" describes this entity so well.

The act of forming the encapsulated "I" occurred during childhood. That part of the "I" was trapped within the developmental conditions of childhood, that is, the period in development when the Self is radically dependent on, as well as radically vulnerable to, the Other. This way of viewing the Self and Others is maintained by that disconnected part of the "I" as it relates to others in the real world or to the parental images in the nether world of the unconscious.

But the psychological conflicts and distortions of Dana's childhood years led to an incomplete development of her intrapsychic world. She had not been able to progress beyond this intermediate, developmental stage of the centrality of the parental figures (both external and internal) to the final step of the "I" as the focus of her existence. As a result, Dana could not achieve full psychological functioning until these still undeveloped stages were in some way brought to fruition. This is where psychotherapy can become the crucial factor in assisting the person.

To understand this better, let us look at it by way of analogy. In the development of the heart of the human fetus, there is a definite progress along these lines: first the heart has a single chamber; then it develops a second, a third, and finally, in the very last months of the mother's pregnancy, its fourth chamber. If these anatomical stages do not progress properly, the infant will be born with its biological survival severely endangered. At times an infant is born with a partially developed four-chambered heart. In this case the wall that constitutes the fourth chamber has not been completed, so the infant is born with an incomplete heart. When this occurs, the oxygenated blood mixes with the unoxygenated blood. Insufficient supplies of oxygen are pumped to the rest of the body. The inefficiency is too great for the child to lead a normal active life. Either the child's continued anatomical development will heal the defect or the underdeveloped organ must be corrected through surgery.

Since the conflicts and oppressive relationships in Dana's childhood curtailed her psychological development, she was unable to surpass the intermediate stage in her psychological growth. The stage of internalization remained the focus of her intrapsychic life. Dana entered the adult world with only a partially developed psychological identity, much like the unfortunate infant. As surgery can correct a deficient heart, psychotherapy can help Dana resolve these inner conflicts by helping her to reclaim the disowned "I" and let go of the Inner Other personae.

The process of incorporating Important Others through internal images intrapsychically represents an important stage in the psychological growth of the Self; it helps in the socialization of the child as well as helping to bring the child to a crystallized awareness of Self. But this process of internalization is meant to be only a temporary stage. A child must experience the freedom and encouragement to move beyond this halfway point in its psychological development. The child who develops neurotic beliefs and ways of behaving, on the other hand, has not been encouraged to travel the road to autonomy.

This child comes to believe, as Dana did, that it is radically dependent on the power of the Important Other to survive. Because it fears that any assertion of its autonomy and self-identity will result in the Important Other's disfavor and ultimate abandonment and because the anticipation of that event is so life-threatening, it rarely takes that step on its own. So the Inner Other remains the central energy of the person, not the "I." The "I" then experiences itself as cut into parts, that is, *disintegrated.* Yet the need for "I" integrity never disappears. With Dana, these disclaimed parts of herself formed the encapsulated Child-Within who occasionally emerged from the recesses of Dana's unconscious psyche to resist the takeover of Dana by the Inner Other. The need for the resistance occurred because, when she gave herself over to the parental values, she lost her Self. She therefore suffered a loss of life from the loss of identity in the capitulation to the Inner Others. At that point, as we saw in the opening multilayered dialogue with Dana, her Child would jump out of her psychic prison temporarily and take over Dana's behavior in defiance of the Inner Others as a way of momentarily preserving the "I" integrity. Immediately, they would clamor for the correction of the situation and punish the culprit. The part of Dana that was allied with the Inner Others because of her mistaken belief in the importance of these internalized forces would slam the Child-Within back in prison. She found herself in an apparently endless cycle of giving herself over to the Inner Others and then momentarily resisting the giving-over through the person of the child-within and its rebellion. This gave way to an irreconcilable psychological tension that was an equivalent to a psychological resistance to self-destruction and fight for life, rather than an acceptance of life through psychological self-identity and integrity as a given and something that didn't have to be fought for.

Boundaries

As I mentioned earlier, there is a discrete developmental period in which the child discovers and works out who it is by using the word "no" at every turn in its interactions with others. A part of what it is doing is testing others to see if it will be allowed to establish its own individual integrity—the breadth and extent of the Self's personal domain. It is important that this process of emerging self-identity be respected by the adults. Because of the psychological significance of the "no" during this period, a child must be given the right to say "no." More often, however, family members are intimidated when the child says "no." They engage in an attempt to overwhelm the child who becomes over-defined and limited.

On the other side of the scale is the necessity for others to respond to the child's "no" negatively if the child is either endangering itself or violating the rights of someone else. Naturally, as a child begins to explore its psychological boundaries both in relationship to others as well as to its own inner inviolability and integrity through the "no," conflicts are bound to arise between the child and the others in its environment. When the child wants to do something that is potentially dangerous or infringes on the rights and needs of others, it is extremely important for the adult to establish its own boundaries (or the boundaries of others) so that the child comes to understand that it *does* have boundaries and limits which are determined by outside circumstances and persons.

A woman I know with a teenage son was distraught when he misused a tape recorder which belonged to her. She had placed her tape recorder in the living room so that the whole family, including herself, could enjoy its use. In the course of time, the tape recorder disappeared into her son's room and was not returned to the living room. She was very upset. I asked her why she didn't demand that the machine be brought back to the common family area. She said she was afraid that she would "hurt" the boy if she made this demand, even though the recorder was rightfully hers to use and regulate. Because she continually has trouble responding to her son in this way, he continually pushed her to get this kind of response. Because he rarely got it, he floundered about without necessary direction. When, however, she began to claim more of what was her own (and stopped interfering with issues that were clearly his) the friction between them lessened and he seemed to be more capable of directing himself.

On the other hand, the parent's definitions of boundaries ceases to be healthy when the parent exerts its will and power in order to flex muscles of psychological authority over the child rather than to help define mutual individualities.

For example, a young mother once came to a session upset that her six-year-old son had reverted to a past habit of sucking his thumb and clutching his highly prized but ragged baby blanket. Because this behavior disturbed her considerably, she had taken strong measures to curtail it by telling him he could engage in that activity only in his room, and that is exactly what he did! He went to his room and sucked his thumb there. Now the mother was upset because the child was generally absent from the main flow of the family.

When we explored the child's behavior and his mother's reaction to it, we discovered that the issue was not what the thumbsucking meant to the boy, but what it meant to the mother: what would the other mothers think of her? The nature of the interaction between the mother and son concerning this thumbsucking issue had become a contest of wills.

This power struggle was clearly exemplified by an incident that occurred one day when the mother and her son went out shopping. As soon as the mother told the child they had to go out, he ran to get his blanket and came back with his thumb in his mouth. My hunch was that the boy's behavior was partly prompted by anxiety about going out. However, when the mother saw the child clutching his blanket and his thumb in his mouth, she tried to get him to stop the behavior. Finally, after cajoling, threatening, and scolding, she realized she had no choice but to take him along with the blanket in one hand and his thumb in his mouth.

Once they got in the car, the boy took his thumb out of his mouth and the blanket fell limp on the car seat. What had suddenly produced this desired behavior in the boy? First, the boy probably felt anxiety about going out, and the blanket and the act of sucking his thumb helped to calm his anxiety; second, psychologically, the boy recognized the power struggle happening between himself and his mother, and he was determined to resist her takeover by continuing the behavior she disapproved of; third, once the mother relinquished her struggle to get the boy to remove his thumb from his mouth and to leave the blanket at home, the boy thought he had won the struggle, and he no longer had the need to clutch the blanket or suck his thumb in lifesaving defiance of her. The initial motivation to carry the blanket and suck his thumb, that is, the boy's inner anxiety, had been forgotten in the power struggle between the boy and his mother, and once the boy thought he had won the struggle, the blanket and his thumb were of no more use.

As the mother and I discussed the incident, she began to see in what ways this occurrence had been important for her own self-understanding. We determined that it was important for her to let go of her overriding concern with what other mothers might think of her, and become more objective about the motivation of her six-year-old's regressive behavior. I suggested to her that she begin responding to the boy's behavior as an indication of some kind of anxiety that the boy was unable to verbalize; furthermore, I recommended that she refrain from punishing the child for his behavior unless it interfered with their interactions in a particular way. In response to this, she related an incident in which the boy's behavior did get in the way of what the two of them were trying to do.

One afternoon she was teaching him how to use scissors by helping him cut out pictures from one of his playbooks. However, her participation was having little impact on the boy because he sat there all the while with his thumb in his mouth and the blanket in the other hand. As usual, she had told the boy to go to his room since his blanket and his thumb were keeping him from engaging in the activity at hand. The boy had done just that, which in turn had upset the mother.

I suggested that rather than treating her son's behavior as a transgression of her clearly expressed rule, she might point out to her son that his behavior was preventing them from accomplishing what they were there to do, which was to learn to use the scissors and play with the playbook. Further, she might express to the child that he had a choice—he could continue to clutch his blanket and suck his thumb, or he could play with the cutouts. The purpose was to make the child believe that the choice was his; in this instance, Mommy was not issuing a dictum that the boy would feel compelled to resist in order to preserve his sense of personal identity and integrity. The conflict of wills would become deflated, and the boy would be able to choose what he thought was best for him at the particular moment. This kind of response from the mother would teach her son that he controlled and was responsible for his own actions.

I went on to propose that the mother resist seeing the child's undesirable behavior as an insult to her capabilities as a mother, and that she recognize the boy's behavior as a sign of an unexpressed inner need. The first step toward a solution of the problem in general would have been to stop the activity and talk specifically about what the boy was feeling.

A couple of weeks later, the mother returned to tell me that she had abandoned the "no blanket, no thumb" rule, and had begun addressing her child's behavior in the ways I had previously suggested. His withdrawal from the rest of the family was disappearing, the thumbsucking was rapidly diminishing, and the blanket was falling into disuse. Her child was beginning to talk freely about his needs and anxieties. She found out that, in fact, there were quite a number of things he was appropriately disturbed about. The family had recently moved and he did not have any familiar peers with whom he could play. In addition, the new home was somewhat isolated, so it was difficult to find and engage peers. Further, she found out that the boy was disturbed about his father's not being around much and his irascibility when he was.

This then brought us to the other side of this dynamic, interpersonal equation, her marriage. By not addressing the reasons for her son's behavior and merely scolding and punishing him, she was not recognizing basic issues in her marriage.

The real issue between this mother and her boy was not whether he sucked his thumb or held his blanket or not, but was one of "I" identity for both the mother and the child. In the mother's mind, if she lost the respect of her peers (other mothers) because her child was demonstrating regressive behavior, her identity as a mother and, ultimately, as a person was severely bruised, so she thought. She initially sought a solution to the threat to her "I" identity by forcing her son to conform so that the other women would not "think" those "bad things" about her.

On the other hand, the boy's "I" identity was being severely threatened by his mother's response to him because she was not responding to some of his deep-seated needs. Instead, the mother's own subconscious agenda was rigidly being forced upon the child.

Luckily for the boy and the mother, she was able to identify her own underlying issues so that she was able to hear what was really troubling him. Because of that, a profound sense of connectedness was established between them. As a result, it appeared that the child was able to establish a sense of security and trust with the mother. Their relationship had been badly ruptured as the boy found his mother an adversary against his striving for "I" identity.

Unfortunately, there are many parents who do not come to terms with their "hidden agendas" as this mother did. Therefore, the sort of thing that was happening between this mother and child can continue unabated, with the struggle for power between the two growing to monumental proportions. Because the parent by definition ultimately has the concentration of power, the child is the loser when the parent doesn't come to terms with its own agendas as this mother did. Dana and Chris were two children for whom this was the case. Because they were, they grew up having internalized the conflict with all the conditions of the parent-child relationship having remained intact. It was this internal conflict that they now lived out on a daily basis as though it were just as real as it was in their childhood.

4

THE STRUGGLE AND CONFLICT IN ACHIEVING INDIVIDUALITY

The Compromises

Prior to the mother's resolution of her underlying problem, the boy was caught in an unresolvable bind. That dilemma he found himself in was the same one Dana and Chris found themselves in when their Important Others had their own unresolved conflicts which they displaced onto Dana and Chris as children. When this happens between any child and parental figure, the problem is the same and the dilemma it raises is also.

The problem it presents to the child is this: "If I am to be in relationship to the other, I must abdicate who I am. If I don't give up my identity, then I will lose my connectedness with the other." The child is then left to make one of two choices, both of which have profound negative psychological and interpersonal ramifications for that developing person.

Essentially, this was the problem and these were the solutions the mother presented to the boy. Since she had erroneously identified the boy's symptoms as the cause of her sense of loss of "I" identity, she was in effect saying to him (somewhat frantically) "You must not be what you are (anxious about real problems and showing the anxiety the way you are through the regressive behavior of the thumbsucking and blanket holding) or else you will suffer my loss because I will not allow you to be in my presence. I will send you to your room unless and until you conform to my expectations of you." Much to the mother's consternation, the boy did make a choice, but not the one she expected. She wanted and expected him to choose to capitulate to her demand that he give up the symptoms (the last hold he had on his sense of "I" identity around these complex and deep-seated issues). Rather, he chose to lose his connectedness with her (and ultimately the rest of the family) and to preserve his sense of identity through the act of rebellion by going to his room. The mother, in turn, was surprised and baffled by his choice because, when she had been presented with the same problem at the same developmental time by her own parents, she made the other choice: to capitulate to their demands, to become other than what she was, in trade for "connectedness" with them.

No matter which choice the child happens to make, neither helps it grow to a full sense of awareness of itself as an "I." If the child "chooses" to capitulate to the other's demand to give up who it is in its experience of itself, as this mother did and as we shall see Dana do, the possibility of affirmation the subject receives through the stimulation of its own experience is lost because it is taught to disown it. Because an entire source of stimulation is lost or radically undermined, the person cannot experience itself as "I am," separate, autonomous, identified, and of value in its own right. That child is left then to seek its identity through the stimulation it finds in the contact with the other. In the meantime the quantitative and qualitative source of stimulation in the experience of Self is lost to it. This is the underlying concept toward understanding Dana's psychological process, and there is a word that summarizes it. Since this choice, the process, and beliefs behind it will be referred to frequently, it will be helpful to label it. Dana's, the mother's, psychological choice has come to be known as the *hysterical compromise*.

The other choice that is available to the child when this dilemma is presented to it by the Important Other, the one chosen by the boy and, as we will see, by Chris, is the *schizoid compromise*. In this choice, the child switches around the source of "I" affirming stimulation it is willing to give up and the one it strives to maintain. Unlike the child who chooses the stimulation of relatedness over the stimulation of its own experience of itself and the world, the child who makes the schizoid choice compromises the sense of stimulation it receives in the experience of relatedness, and chooses the stimulation it experiences in holding tightly to its own experience of itself and the other.

But, as in the hysterical choice, it loses the quantitative extent of that source of stimulation as well as the qualitative difference of the two types of experiences.

No matter which of these two types of choices any person makes to solve this apparent psychological dilemma, the person is left with a stimulation void. If the subject makes the hysterical choice, it experiences itself as a hollow core that it believes it can fill up arbitrarily with everybody else's experience but its own. This, of course, is a deception because no one else's experience can be "my" own. Therefore the psychological void that is created by the subject's failure to claim itself in its own experience and to substitute everyone else's will never fill that void and in fact, as we shall see, will only exacerbate it. The schizoid choice leaves the subject with a deep and apparently unresolvable sense of interpersonal void—loneliness.

There is a way out of this dilemma, as there is a third choice available to the subject who is caught in it. Luckily for the boy, his mother, in working through *her* problem, was able to present it to him while he was a child. The choice was "You do not have to capitulate. I will try to understand what is happening to you and let you make choices that are appropriate for you to make. The choices you make to affirm your sense of Self will not alienate us." Dana and Chris have had to understand that the way they experienced their Important Others relating to them as children (and as they probably did relate to them) was: "Either you capitulate to me or you lose me," and this is not a choice that everyone presented to them.

Dana

When I first saw Dana she was a well-dressed woman in her early fifties. She had raised a daughter and now was pursuing a career of her own. She was the prime force behind a business venture which included her husband and brother-in-law as partners, and she was determined to make this venture succeed. Although she complained about being depressed at times, for the most part she spoke with some sense of self-assurance. The longer we worked together and the more her deeper emotional problems surfaced, the more her self-assurance seemed to disappear. It was a veneer, and when Dana could no longer expend the tremendous amounts of energy required to maintain it, it cracked, split, and finally gave way to depression—a depression that was characterized by an overwhelming immobilization, so complete in its effectiveness that at times she found it impossible to get out of bed. At the moment she woke her mind would be flooded with thoughts of self-doubt and recrimination. The more she thought about what she had to do during the day, the more intense the thoughts became. As this continued her condition grew worse. Her body twisted and bent, her face contorted in expressions of fear—a fear that seemed to be boundless, pervading her body from within and engulfing her from without. The simplest decisions were beyond her reach and any possibility of articulating her thoughts and feelings was lost in the confusion. In the end this seemingly self-assured woman, intelligent, successful, and "mature," lay there paralyzed from fear like a vulnerable child.

Dana's relationship with her husband echoed her extreme passivity and dependence. Over the years she consulted him on every decision she made, even to whether she should take an aspirin for a headache. When she spoke to him her voice sounded more like the voice of a whiney child. And, like a child, she demanded that he hold her for long periods of time, especially in the morning. When she found it more difficult to go to work, she would plead with him to stay home and hold her. At the beginning, her husband gave in. But it continued and soon smacked up against the reality of running a business. Dana's husband couldn't stay home indefinitely, so he stopped complying with her demands. Dana panicked.

Dana was the motivating force toward making her partnership with her husband and brother-in-law successful. Although these depressions were very long-lasting, they occasionally lifted. When they did, her "self-assurance" reappeared. Interestingly, her demands for physical attention then dropped off sharply, at which times, she admitted (and her husband complained) that she kept him at a cool distance: she didn't need or want anything from him, nor would she give him anything. He couldn't get any affection from her during these periods and it seemed as though her original need to be smothered by him physically, emotionally, and psychologically was replaced by a need to be isolated—walled off from the world so that, in effect, she could not touch or be touched by others. During these periods I also found her distant and aloof in our relationship.

Dana is a person with keen psychological insight. While we worked together Dana was perceptive and remarkably objective in relation to her unmarried twenty-six-year-old daughter. She recognized many of her own conflicts mirrored in her daughter, and showed appropriate concern. But she did not interfere with her daughter's life. She did not understand or agree with many aspects of her daughter's lifestyle, but she never became overly involved in them. In this respect she was not typical of women with the same middle-class background. This quality seemed incongruous with her own preoccupation with what others thought about her behavior and values. For some reason, this particular attitude was exempt from an undermining scrutiny.

The Conflict—Contact vs. Integrity

From childhood on, Dana maintained contact with her Important Others, and ultimately all Others, by disowning her own identity and splitting herself into disparate parts. To split off and disown those parts was not to extinguish their existence, however, for they continued to dwell in the recesses of her psyche and to wage battle with her parental images. They did this through both active rebellion and the passive resistance of her helplessness that took an extreme psychological and physical toll on Dana.

It is difficult to appreciate the extent and the radical nature of this splitting apart and disowning. Following is a portion of a session showing the extent to which Dana was not present to herself, not only through what she was saying but through the way she was saying it. The loss of her sense of identity clearly revolves around her need for contact with others versus her need to maintain her "I" identity:

Dana: Why do I say "you"? . . . You see I don't want to say "I." I want it in the category of everybody so that I'm not . . . it's

> not happening to me. . . . Well, it's a denial in a certain way and it also puts me with another group so that I'm not alone. People. But it's happening to me. I don't know what's happening to anybody else. I really can't ever know.
>
> I think it doesn't make me feel so alone if I say "you." Then other people experience it. But they're not really. If you decide . . . if you say to yourself, "I'm not consciously . . ." I don't know. The "you" . . . there are other people that are . . . that feel this way at times, it's just not . . . it's just not "you." That doesn't explain anything. That's not a unique thing happening to you . . . other people . . . but it is unique. I don't want it happening to me, I guess. First of all, I don't want it happening. [Sigh] I feel weak, that I can't determine my own existence.

It is apparent that as she is talking she feels a deep sense of confusion about who she is. Is she talking about herself, or about people in general when she uses "you"? She doesn't know whether her experience is unique or not, nor does she even know if it's her *own* experience. "Well, it's a denial in a certain way and it puts me with another group so that I'm not alone. People."

Within this particular statement we are able to see the conflict: "If I make it so that it is not my experience but everybody else's then I will not be alone, that is, I can be with people. But to be with people, others, I must disown my experience (make it others'). I, therefore, must disown myself, that is, give up my personal identity. I give up my personal identity by disowning my experience as it is happening. Therefore I cannot say 'I' but only 'you' since my experience has to be yours and not mine."

She then immediately proceeded to use the pronoun "you" ("if you decide," "If you say to yourself. . . .") thereby disowning herself as she was talking about disowning herself. With this act she was unwittingly complying with the command of her Inner Others: "If you are to be with people, you must become them and give up yourself." And Dana had just previously admitted, "It does not make me feel so alone if I say 'you.'" There it was! She believed that the only means of making contact with people lay in the act of disowning herself.

She went on to explore the reason why she paid such close attention to the dictum of her Inner Others. "I don't want it happening to me!" she exclaimed, meaning she neither wanted to own her own feelings, participate in her own activities, decision-making processes, nor even in her own therapy. This was revealed later in the session when she said:

> You know, I've lost sight of . . . I forget what we've discussed here. When I listen to a tape what I've said comes back to me. It's a kind of reinforcement. . . . The little hints you give about what I'm feeling. . . . The little ways you try to get me to react. . . . I forget them sometimes. . . . I can also hear my own voice—how it is at times when I don't feel well, which is most of the time— real dreary. . . . I also can't even. . . . Well, it's like another person. . . . You don't recognize your own voice. You think it's another person. I don't know. . . . I don't recognize me and other people have said that they don't recognize me either. . . . I *do* seem like somebody else.

Within the therapeutic context Dana consistently functioned under the psychic rule of her Inner Others. Consequently, therapy did not provide her with an experience of inner fitness and self-understanding, but instead became a vehicle by which she could continue to disown her Self while struggling to understand her compulsion to do so. So formidable was the impact of her Inner Others on her fragile identity that not only did her friends often fail to recognize "Dana," but she was often unable to recognize herself! Further, she was unable to assimilate the insights which emerged from the therapeutic process into her self-identity. All insights remained mine, not hers. They existed for her because I (therapist-authority figure) had weighted certain of her statements with importance, not because she was able to connect what she heard with her inner experiences. As the preceding monologue has demonstrated, Dana often forgot what she had said in a previous therapy session. The only way she was able to hang onto significant discoveries made in the session was through listening to the tape. But even then, the insights remained *my* insights, *my* words, *my* values, and consequently their effect on Dana's buried sense of Self was negligible. Since Dana's Inner Others refused to allow her to function for herself in any other aspect of her life, it was not surprising that their ubiquitous control would reach out to sabotage the therapeutic process as well.

Dana had explicitly stated: "I must give up my Self in order to make contact with others." Initially, Dana's hysterical compromise was evolved as a means of making contact with Important Others, which would thereby affirm her own identity. But the irony of the hysterical compromise is that in its provision of contact with others it subverts rather than affirms the "I" identity. This pattern of relating is indeed a compromise—a profound one which creates a grave psychological dilemma. Should one give up one's Self in order to feel contact with others, or should one give up contact with others in order to preserve an inner identity?

Chris

When Chris first came to me for help, he was in his early forties and, consistent with his Irish-Catholic upbringing, he insisted on calling me "Father." He spoke so softly that at times he'd fade into a whisper. Very early on in his treatment I recognized how this tied in with his inability to accept his own worth and value as a human being.

He came to me to deal with specific problems he was having. He had been involved in a complicated, unrewarding, and destructive relationship with a married man. Initially, the relationship began and continued because of the advances made by this other man. Even though Chris lived a life of intense isolation and was reluctant to get involved with anyone, the man was persistent and, after a while, Chris discovered that he enjoyed having a friend with whom he could share his time and thoughts, so he began to respond. When he finally became emotionally involved, the other man pulled away.

Chris was confused. He was also very angry but, instead of getting in touch with his anger and expressing the reasons for it, he repressed it so that it eventually took the form of guilt and self-abuse that resulted in severe depression. For several months I helped Chris through the decision-making process that finally led to Chris's breaking up this damaging relationship. He was also beginning to acknowledge the anger that he felt towards this man and, maybe for the first time in his life, he was expressing this anger and not turning it inwards against himself.

In time it became clear to me that Chris had had a very intense relationship with his mother, who could only be described as demanding, demeaning, and sadistic. In fact, Chris's relationship with his mother sounded incredibly similar to the relationship he had with this man. As we explored his personal history, it was apparent from the start that Chris's mother had consistently undermined his attempts to succeed in life.

Chris's three brothers had spent most of their adult life in prison. Chris tried to make his own way by getting a good education: he entered a seminary during high school to become a priest. But although Chris was well above average intelligence, his mother would constantly "remind" him just how stupid he was. When he entered the seminary, she did everything she could to sabotage his image of himself as a priest. Even the decision to leave was taken out of his hands when she went to the rector and complained that she had no one to take care of her. The rector called Chris in and suggested that his greater duty was to leave to take care of his mother.

So he left the seminary and became a teacher. She let him know her thoughts on that matter too: "You, a teacher?!" he recalled her saying to him; "What could *you* teach anyone?" Despite the fact that he thoroughly enjoyed his work and he especially enjoyed working with children, he finally gave up teaching.

Even though his mother made such incredible demands on him, he was drawn back to her time and again, like a magnet, giving in to her each time. He conformed more and more to his mother's opinion of himself. He isolated himself more drastically and in the end took a job as a doorman in an apartment building on the graveyard shift—from ten at night to six in the morning. Not only was the isolation drastic but the change was drastic, too. While Chris set the highest standards for himself to begin with—selecting career goals that were intellectually stimulating, emotionally rewarding, and in the mainstream of life—as he gave in to his mother's view of himself, he wound up in a position where there was no intellectual stimulation whatsoever, which included little or no relating with others on any level, and which was far from the mainstream of life.

During the time he spent with me he began to appreciate just how damaging his relationship with his mother had become; he therefore decided to see her less. He had come to realize that no matter what he said or did, he could expect only demands and abuse from her and there were no indications that this would ever change.

Also, the longer we worked together, the more I came to realize that Chris was not only intelligent but sensitive as well. He frequently expressed a great deal of warmth toward people either in the interpersonal relationships he described to me or in his interaction with members of a group he joined at my invitation. In fact, I asked Chris to join this group so that I could observe the way he related to others firsthand. In the group I wasn't relying solely on his accounts of events; I could now compare his perceptions of how he related to others with what I observed as his patterns of relating in the group. And, if I did observe a pattern that led to a problem in relating, I could bring it to his attention immediately. With Chris, as with most people, this immediacy was invaluable because, as we discussed it, his thoughts and feelings about the event were more readily available to him than they might have been days or weeks later. And Chris discovered that when his thoughts and feelings were readily accessible, it was easier for him to examine them and even to draw some conclusions about them.

Chris's participation in the group acted like a catalyst in uncovering his basic problem. Chris had little trouble genuinely feeling and expressing warmth towards others. No, his problem stemmed from his inability to accept the warmth that others extended towards him. For reasons which we'll explore later on, Chris did not believe that anyone could feel or think anyting positive about him.

Another aspect of Chris's personality was manifested in the group's interaction: his wonderful sense of humor and charming way with words, his sensitivity to people and events. He was a keen observer of events and could describe even a subtle interaction that might elude most of the other members of the group. He also responded with care and concern to another's need for help.

He was well-liked by the group members but he was unable to accept, receive, or at times even hear any positive feedback. His inability to accept warmth was based on an internal assumption that he wasn't worth caring for. His diminished sense of self-worth pushed him into a world of extreme isolation. As already mentioned, his working hours kept him out of the mainstream of social life. But consider too that he had no fellow workers and that his contact with the building's tenants was brief and impersonal simply because at that time of night most people in the building were either too tired or too drunk to offer more than a cursory "Good night." Not infrequently he'd have to put up with the abuse of a crackpot or a tenant who had had a bit too much to drink. In this way he not only acted out, but reinforced his sense of worthlessness and isolation.

But it wasn't only his working time that indicated these attitudes. He lived alone in an apartment in a section of the city where there are more factories and warehouses than homes. He had no friends to speak of, although at times he'd refer to one or two people as "friends." Yet it was disconcertingly apparent, even to Chris at times, that in reality these people used him without connecting with him as a person. They only called on him when they needed money or when their own loneliness was so unbearable that they needed to talk *at* him as a respite to relieve it. Chris made excuses for them but ultimately he knew that they would not have been there if he had needed them.

The first dream he related to me depicted accurately how Chris viewed himself in his interpersonal world:

> I dreamed I was on a cot in a big, empty room. Off, over to one side, are two figures, statues. [He begins to sob.] Strewn all around the cot is broken glass. I couldn't have gotten out of bed even if I wanted to.

Given this self-image there's little wonder why he chose to isolate himself. As we'll discover later on, however, the resolution of Chris's problem did not come in breaking off the sadistic relationships with his mother, with his male friend, or with his other "friends." He first had to become aware of the internal dialogue that persisted wherever he went, independently of these or any relationships—the dialogue that created his self-image and led him to behave according to it, destroying everything in Chris's life that didn't conform to it and insuring that all events and people in his life would support that low self-image. Once he became conscious of the dialogue and its devastating consequences, he could then take definite steps to overcome its strictures and finally change it.

The Other as Enemy

Chris believed that, to be in relationship, he must give himself over to the Other who is more powerful than he, and he was generally unwilling to do this. Dana saw her Inner Others as absolutely essential to her psychological survival and well-being. From this perspective, she was willing to give up her own identity in order to preserve the stimulation of the interpersonal relationships. From that she derived her identity but lost the sense of substance about herself that was gained through an acknowledgment and honoring of her own feelings, needs, and perceptions. Whenever Chris contemplated entering into relationship, he still was confronted with his original interpersonal experience that, if he expected to be in relationship, he, like Dana, had to capitulate before the Other. Rather than make the choice to capitulate before the Other, as Dana did, he chose to remove himself from relationship and to draw his stimulation from his own inner resources.

Chris had chosen the schizoid compromise. From that, he was able to develop a strong sense of his own personal identity. But, given the relational content, he was up against the same kind of dilemma Dana was. By choosing the conditions of the Important Others ("become who I want you to be or else I will abandon you"), Dana gained interpersonal stimulation but lost the stimulation of her own inner Self. Her sense of personal experience was greatly weakened due to the loss of her Self as a core that received the stimulation. Chris, on the other hand, gained the stimulation that was derived from the inner Self. He was able to build up a relatively strong sense of Self because he was not willing to give himself over to the Other. Because he made this kind of psychological choice, he was able to look at external reality, come to his conclusions about it, hold onto them, and develop a rich conceptual and image life.

On the other hand, though, Chris lived in psychological isolation. The result was a life that was interpersonally impoverished because the whole realm of interpersonal stimulation was lost to him. For a time he looked to fill this void by developing his inner life in the areas mentioned above. Ultimately, though, the fundamental loneliness began to seep into his bones. When he started experiencing that, he could no longer compensate for the radical loneliness he felt through reading, artwork, or anything else. He then sought out therapy to find out what was wrong.

This view of the interpersonal world as one populated by hostile others began with his mother who apparently *was* extremely critical, overpowering, and overbearing. Not only did he describe childhood memories of his mother in this way, but he also included modern events that happened within days of our sessions. I realize that whenever I am listening to someone's perception of someone else, the account is open to distortions. On the other hand, though, I've made a practice of meeting the parents of the persons I'm working with (whenever possible). Although I never met his mother, more often than not, when I hear about parents over a long course of history who are described as Chris described his mother, I'm surprised by the accuracy in the description by the offspring of the personality traits of the parent. If the kind of parenting Chris described is what he experienced, it is no wonder that he shrank from interpersonal relationship. But even if that is what he perceived as the basis for relationship, it is no wonder he pulled back.

Because this was his interpersonal experience, he felt a profound sense of terror whenever he anticipated entering into a relationship with someone. Since he internalized his mother's response to him and applied what had happened in that specific relationship to all relationships, he generally chose to cut himself off from others to preserve himself from the original pain he felt when he engaged the original other, his mother. The result was that any form of contact with another that threatened to develop into something other than a shallow acquaintanceship was met by a seemingly impenetrable psychological armor; this was not a response to the outside world but *was* a response to a very real inner world inhabitated by his internal mother who said to him: "You are nothing but refuse, so don't expect anything good from anybody because you don't deserve it!"

A psychologically threatened child chooses one of these two patterns of relating as a means of coping with the demands of the interpersonal environment. By adulthood, however, the choice, which was based on assumptions and the realities of childhood that the Important Other was infinitely powerful as well as irreplaceable, no longer applies to the present existence. The continuation of one or both of these patterns of relating distorts and overvalues the importance and power of others involved in one's life rather than acknowledging the power of the Self. It is then that the patterns become neurotic, because they are based on outmoded assumptions and thereby no longer help a person to cope successfully with present-day relationships.

A child, of course, does not choose one of these patterns of relating excusively. In fact, most people vacillate between the two. For example, when a person has been basically functioning out of the hysterical compromise, the pain caused by the disappearance of the sense of Self becomes overwhelming. Usually, that person then moves into a pattern of relating that prohibits interaction with others; he attempts to recoup an inner sense of integrity by not giving the Self over in interaction with others—the schizoid compromise. However, with time, the loneliness from a self-imposed emotional psychological and/or physical isolation becomes unbearable, and the person resumes relating to others, but in the same self-dismissing manner as before—and the cycle begins again.

Though individuals may vacillate from one pattern of relating to the other, it does happen that they habitually relate one way more than the other. Dana spent most of her time disowning herself in the presence of others, but she did enter periods when she summoned her sense of Self in such a way that she was propelled into great loneliness. Chris spent most of his time in a state of physical and psychological isolation from others. Occasionally he would make moves to enter into close relationship with another person, but only tentatively. Soon the fear of losing his hard-won identity would overwhelm him and he would break the bonds of closeness with another as the only available means of preserving his precious sense of Self.

In the following session, Chris's ambivalence about relationships becomes manifest:

Jack: How are you today?

Chris: Not bad. . . . I don't know where to begin. Yesterday, we were talking a little bit about my expectations about what an emotional and sexual relationship ought to be. Maybe that's a decent place to start. [He laughs.]

Uhh . . . my expectation is that I ought to feel strong feelings for a woman, both emotionally and sexually; and also in terms of, you know, wanting to be with her . . . and having her be somebody I respect and like to be with—emotionally like to be with. And that I really want to make love with her and not just have sex.

Jack: Where did the word "ought" come from?

Chris: Pardon me?

Jack: You said, "What an emotional relationship *ought* to be." And, "I *ought* to feel strong feelings for a woman." You could have used the word "want."

Chris: Well, the fact is that I *do* want to.

Jack: But that isn't what you said.

Chris: I said "ought" because I don't . . . because that's the way it . . . that's the way it is. . . . If I weren't . . . in the life situation that I'm in, if I hadn't fucked it all up along with, you know, in response to some . . . in response to my mother and father . . . then that would be the natural process of the thing for me or anybody. And yes, I do want that.

[Chris had not yet answered my question about where the word "ought" came from. His explanation was very confused; however, it was laden with guilt concerning the way he has "fucked up" his life right from the start, with his mother and father. His explanation also contained the word "should." The following was an interchange between us which revealed the underlying process from which the words "ought" and "should" originate.]

Chris: So there's something in me saying, "You must love," and I'm saying, "No, you can't make me love. If I really do love I'm going to be eaten alive." In effect.

Jack: What would happen if you admitted loving feelings for someone?

Chris: If I admitted. . . . Something says that it would mean I would be giving in. I see it as being trapped, bound. [Pause] You know, there's something that has a great deal of effect on me. There's a description of the Rosenbergs . . . Julius is being pulled away from his wife's cell before he's about to be executed. That scene almost destroyed me. . . . There's a fantasy that I have . . . where I'm in a similar situation . . . but I'd never let *anybody kill me.* [This is said between clenched teeth.]

Jack: What does that fantasy mean to you?

Chris: That's what I thought was going to happen to me in childhood. And I'm not going to let them.

Jack: As a child, what tools did you have to prevent that?

Chris: As a child, nothing.

Jack: With the exception of what?

Chris: Denial.

Jack: The only thing you could do was to not let them get at the core of you. And then you built walls around your core. That was the only thing they couldn't get to and you knew it.

Chris: [Sobbing.] That's too young to do that!

Jack: It's always too young to do that.

The first hint that Chris's problem centered around an inability to express love came to me when he used the words "ought" and "should." To speak of loving as an obligation that one "ought to" fulfill inhibits the naturalness of the expression and puts it in a moral context in which there are implicit rights and wrongs, in which one is either guilty or not guilty, good or bad. If a person does not love as prescribed either by himself or another he has failed to fulfill an obligation, and a judgment is made. Chris expressed his inner decree, "You must love!" and indeed he wanted to love, yet he refused to allow himself to do so, because he saw it as an act of submission and giving himself to takeover by others.

In another session, Chris described himself as being fortified within a castle, peering out above the top of a massive wall. Other people with whom he felt obligated to maintain relationships, including me, were kept outside the walls of his castle. We would not be allowed inside because of his tremendous fear that we would force him to surrender his identity. His psychological fortress was constructed of a childhood perception of his parents as potential conquerors of his sense of "I." Chris's position within his psychic castle had become the vantage point from which he viewed the world.

Because of the nature of his childhood experience in relation to others, Chris had formed an inner world in which all others were viewed as dangerous enemies. I myself, and members of the group to which he belonged, were seen as adversaries who had to be defied. There were, however, heavy prices Chris paid for maintaining his secure position within his castle: a crippling fear of the power of others to vanquish his identity; the relentless and exhausting compulsion to be always on the defensive when dealing with people; and the consequent feeling of abject loneliness.

Chris was caught in a psychological limbo. The parental voice was constantly demanding that he love, but the act of loving was perceived as a capitulation to the demands of the presumably more powerful other. To preserve his identity he allowed no one to touch him, but Chris's child within was angry that he could not feel the love of another without feeling the threat of being consumed psychologically. The child within was always in the position of weakness and vulnerability in relation to others. Because his anger was "bad," he was kept out of sight. If the anger was made evident to another, the child within thought he would be forced to give it up and that meant capitulation to another's demands, which was tantamount to committing suicide. . . . When we worked with Chris in a group process, often I or the group were the objects of his anger. The anger he felt toward me and the group members was generally acted out in sullen silence and physical withdrawal from us. Only occasionally would he erupt with verbal charges toward us that didn't bear up to the evidence of who we were in relation to him. Usually, they simply represented demands that were being placed on him from within, which were then projected onto us.

The reservoir of anger within him was enormous. He kept it pent up because, when he was a child, he had thought that his anger was unacceptable and his experience was that he would be overwhelmed by the other if he displayed any anger. One aspect of the overwhelmingness of this was his memory of how his mother would grab him when he was angry and tickle him until he laughed to the point of breathlessness. Through this and other kinds of responses to his anger, he had come to believe that he did not have a right to be angry and would be overwhelmed by the other if he did dare to reveal it. His anger towards me and the group covered up enormous fear of us.

By holding onto his anger, Chris believed that he was maintaining his identity; his anger had become equated with his "I." What had initially served as a defense against the loss of his "I" to the demands of powerful figures had now come to represent identity itself. Further, the repressed but very intense anger had become the major source of stimulation from his emotional life. To give up the anger would be to lose that source of stimulation, to give up life itself.

Chris's anger constituted his very Self, yet he thought that his anger was ugly. Because of this correlation, Chris believed that he was basically unlovable. The purpose of keeping people at a great distance was to keep others from seeing how ugly he "really" was. He would not allow them the opportunity to reject him; he rejected them first. Chris desperately tried to maintain his "I" identity, but his defensive tactics kept him from experiencing the major way in which the "I" is affirmed: through positive relationships with others.

Part III

ACTIVITY AND CONTROL BY THE INNER OTHERS

5

THE INTRAPSYCHIC TAKEOVER

At this point, we have established the reality of the presence of the internalized Others; how the developing child creates them and why; and what happens when the model, the parental figures, from which the child molds these images is inappropriate and dysfunctional. Dana's and Chris' lives were altered radically because they possessed within them demanding, demeaning, attacking, criticizing, judgmental, and punishing Inner Others. The politics of the personae within their inner worlds was highly complex, and we will now explore them in some detail.

My Name Is Legion, for We Are Many

As Dana and I groped our way through the realm of the Inner Other as it revealed itself through the "you" form of address and the concomitant rebellion of the child within, many aspects of Dana's depression and the symptoms that sprang from it were somewhat alleviated. Nevertheless, we had reached an impasse as other facets, other psychological dysfunctions remained untouched and unresolved.

She was having, in fact, more difficulty in getting out of bed in the morning and going to work. To help her cope with this difficult task, she had begun increasingly to enlist Bob's help. It was clear, however, that it was too time-consuming for him. He frequently was late for work himself. In addition, because she could depend on him, she did not confront whatever kept her from accomplishing these morning tasks. Therefore, the three of us (Bob, Dana, and myself) had, in a previous session, decided that Dana would proceed with these tasks on her own without turning to Bob for assistance. Dana agreed to this. She, however, articulated a great deal of fear about it, because of the tremendous effort it would take on her part. She did agree about her overdependence on Bob, but had difficulty getting a handle on whatever was causing the problem.

On her own, she did manage to get out of bed and make it to work. In the session in which she described her internal struggle, the underlying reason for her previous lack of success unveiled itself. Not only was she being ordered about from within, but the orders were often contradictory, which served to exacerbate her already intense confusion and resultant immobilization.

> Dana: He *stayed* home . . . and was distressed about it. And I was distressed too. Yet I want him there! So there you were. Mixed up. Good spot to be in, right? "Don't go shopping! You're not going to feel well. You're going to be sick in the store." But I went! I didn't get sick in the store. Do I have to fight every battle? "What do you want to go to therapy for?" So exhausting!

[Later in the session.]

> And you can control me if I'm sick. I'm not strong when I'm sick. I shake. I think I'm sick! I think there are pains in my stomach, I think I'm sick. I keep telling myself, "I'm not sick!" And then again, "But you must be sick. You must be if you feel that way. You don't want to get out of bed in the morning, you must be sick. You don't have anything to live for." You keep telling me. I do! There must be another world beside this one. Another life.

[Still later in the session.]

> Makes me guilty all day. "Got a pain in your stomach because you are guilty. If you had gone to work you wouldn't have a pain in your stomach. Guilty!" I'm not guilty! Stop twisting me around! "Don't go to therapy, you're not getting anywhere. You're wasting your time. You don't do what you are told. You don't try hard enough. What's Jack going to say when he sees you? You're not getting anywhere after all this time."

It was clear that she was receiving contradictory demands. On the one hand, a "you" voice tells her she is sick and she must stay home in bed. Yet following quickly on that is another "you" voice that says if she hadn't listened to the other voice, she wouldn't have become sick and, because she did listen, the pain she felt in her stomach was really guilt. No wonder she was confused and immobilized!

Until this point in Dana's therapy she had given the name of "Father" to her internal voice because much of what she heard from inside her reminded her of her father, who was demanding, judgmental, never satisfied. But maybe this was an oversimplification. After all, Dana had more than one parental figure. "Could it be," I asked myself, "that Dana had formed more than one Inner Other from her parental figures of childhood? And could they, perhaps, offer conflicting messages, expectations, and orders?"

As a result of observing the conflicting demands and counterdemands and the questions and hypotheses they raised, I began a process of reviewing her childhood history with her. The review brought me to some astonishing conclusions!

Dana was the firstborn. Eighteen months following Dana's birth, a sister was born; and roughly every year and a half after that another child was born until there were seven. Dana's mother was an emotionally and sexually naive young woman, quite ignorant about child-raising and unaware of many aspects of Dana's pre- and post-natal care. Dana suffered from a number of illnesses during her infancy, the first of which occurred when her mother's amniotic sac burst shortly before the expected time of her delivery. Oblivious to the signals of critical developments during pregnancy, the young woman failed to alert a doctor and as a result Dana was born several days late and in critical condition. Later on, Dana's mother developed a mammary infection that restricted the flow of milk to her nursing infant. Again, the period before this dysfunction was corrected was needlessly protracted. The infant Dana had lost a considerable amount of weight before her mother sought medical attention.

When Dana was approximately two years old and her sister about six months, the family moved to a boarding house owned and managed by her father's aunt. Here Dana's mother was enlisted by the aunt to cook, clean, and do laundry for the boarders. Her immaturity and lack of preparation for motherhood had already hindered this young woman's ability to care for Dana; it is not hard to imagine how infrequently she was able to give motherly attention while functioning as a fulltime housekeeper. Further, there was a great deal of fighting in the household because Dana's mother was overworked by her aunt-in-law and resented her husband's indifference to her complaints.

A child of Dana's age naturally demanded a lot of attention. Long workdays, resentment, and family arguments do not leave a mother much time or energy for two very young children. Dana, as the oldest child, was undoubtedly expected to need less attention than her infant sister. Dana was probably left alone a good deal of the time and had to fill most of her own needs.

Whenever Dana felt ill, however, all of this changed. Almost all of the occasions when Dana recalled receiving her mother's attention and care centered upon illnesses she had. As long as Dana was sick, her mother was very solicitous, and Dana remembered basking in the warm glow of her mother's concern during these times. Events between parent and child and the messages inherent in them are psychologically assimilated by the child and an Inner Other image emerges within the psyche. Keeping this in mind, it can readily be understood that at an early age Dana had made a psychological association between illness and her mother's love, just as Mary had made the negative association between the constant monitoring all afternoon from her mother and disowning her spontaneity and playfulness. Seemingly for Dana, the only time her mother loved and cared for her was when she was sick. Illness, then, became a desired state. It brought with it a promise of the deeply missed maternal attention. She kept this belief alive into adulthood by means of that earlier internalization. Internal Mother said, "You must be sick in bed if you are going to be loved and cared for," and Dana complied—with nausea, colitis, and other ailments.

However, to understand the counterdemand, "You are guilty because you didn't go to work (You should have gone to work. You are really faking it)," we must acknowledge the presence of a second Inner Other, the image of Dana's great-aunt. This woman, who exploited Dana's mother and was the cause of much family tension, was a tyrannical figure in Dana's young eyes. Dana remembered her frustration at her constant inability to please the aunt. She favored Dana's younger sister, and no matter how hard Dana tried to emulate her, she always failed in the eyes of her aunt. As a part of Dana's need for motherly attention, she learned to use sickness as a way of achieving it. Her aunt rightly but cruelly accused her of faking the sickness. This is what Dana had internalized from her aunt, and this is what we were hearing that day. Upon closer examination of Dana's monologue, however, the presence of a third internal speaker becomes evident, making Dana's internal conflict a free-for-all between *three* psychic authorities! The demands and counterdemands seemed to revolve around Dana's being sick or not and whether to get out of bed. Then, however, she heard from inside, "You're wasting your time! You don't do what you're told! You don't try hard enough. What's he (Jack) going to say when he sees you? You're not getting anywhere (in therapy) after all this time!" This seemed to be a shift away from the sickbed conflict. And it certainly was.

When Dana and I began to explore this particular attack and others similar to it, she remembered her father hurling those criticisms at her on frequent occasions. For example, when "helping" her with her studies, he would burst into a critical tirade if Dana was "too slow" or failed to answer a question to his satisfaction. When this happened, she was "stupid, didn't pay attention, and was a hopeless student." Since her father worked part-time with her in her husband's business, she was still the object of this same type of hypercritical accusation. These same types of attacks were then assimilated and incorporated into her psyche in the form of an authoritarian father voice.

The reason for Dana's physical, emotional, and psychological paralysis now had a clarity it never had before. Not only did she have an inner voice that undermined her experience and her concept of Self by leveling impossible demands and charges at her, but she had three distinct voices, Mother, Aunt, and Father, who were often at odds with each other regarding the demands they made on Dana. No wonder she ended up paralyzed.

The Parental Values

Dana's assimilation of her mother's proposition, "You must be sick in bed if you are going to be loved," contained within it the implication that Dana had to be in an overly dependent relationship to the other through illness if she was to receive caring, warmth, and affection. Conversely, though, when Dana was feeling well, she also had come to assume unconsciously that a loving response from significant others outside of the context of dependent sickness was not forthcoming. But the need for affection and caring is not over when one leaves childhood, and it continues beyond the time one is sick. Because of the message she received implicitly from her mother during childhood, she had come to believe that her craving for those emotional responses was irrelevant. Therefore, during her healthy periods she was compelled to deny this need because she didn't think she could have it fulfilled.

Bob would confirm this, remarking that Dana seemed to make it difficult for him to experience physical and emotional closeness with her when she was feeling well. When we explored this with Dana, she said that during her healthy times, she felt "strong" and did not think that she really needed the warmth and affection she pursued so avidly when she was ill. At such times, she viewed any awareness or articulation of an emotional or physical need for affection as a childish need and a sign of weakness. This was the period in which she entered her schizoid phase. The pendulum, however, would quickly swing back to where Dana was compelled to be weak and powerless before others, to be hysterical.

This inner belief was a response both to her Internal Mother and to her Aunt. To consider the need for affection in any form as a sign of childishness and weakness obviously came from the Internal Aunt whose roots were in the historical-aunt who wouldn't allow her as a child to seek out affection through sickness. In addition, she was unable to recognize the need for affection from others during those "well" times because she was led to believe through the Internal Mother whose roots were also in history that it would not be forthcoming anyway. Because of the interaction of these two internal persons, Dana was unable to separate being sick and receiving affection and warmth. Furthermore, affection was connected with the pain of sickness, and radical dependency on the Other, as well as with physical and emotional vulnerability. The result was that, during the very time when she was able to receive and give love as an integral person, in a positive and nourishing way, she was deprived of it. Thus, when she began to experience the emotional poverty that grew out of those internalized beliefs, she was plummeted back into ill health, vulnerability and weakness. Reception of affection carried with it the connotation of weakness and vulnerability. Certainly, this was a terrible set of compromises for anyone to have to make. Dana, however, did respond to the needs of others. She was more capable of giving care than of receiving it: further internalization of the maternal belief system.

As the oldest child, Dana had not only been frequently left alone to attend to her own needs, but she had been expected to care for and look after her younger siblings as well. Through the act of caring for the younger children, Dana could attain some degree of recognition from her mother. As an adult, therefore, Dana was able to achieve a degree of internal satisfaction by caring for the needs of others. But neither as a child nor as an adult was Dana able to claim for herself her outgoing concern for others; she could not warrant love and recognition for simply being Dana, a caring individual, but only as her mother's compliant daughter. During one session Dana referred to this conflict: "You know, if the belligerent child in me said she wouldn't help my mother, and if *I* listened to her and didn't help out, I wouldn't be able to forgive myself."

To achieve emotion and psychological maturity, Dana had to let go of the Internal Mother and claim her inner intrinsic worth as a person so that her caring responses to others flowed out of a sense of that inner richness. In the other order of things, she sought her worth because *others* had a positive and accepting response to her and not because that was her experience of herself. With that as the order for her, she could never have a sense that she existed separately from others; she lived out her existence connected to others with an emotional and psychological umbilical cord.

The historical roots of this kind of interplay between Dana and her mother were confirmed in the present day by the following interaction Dana had with her mother one Saturday:

Mother: I want to go to eight o'clock mass tomorrow. Will you take me?

Dana: I've planned to go to the eleven o'clock. Why don't you have Dad or Mary [the next sister after her, who lived upstairs with the parents] take you?

Mother: You know your father won't get out of bed until nine. And you know I can never get your sister to drive me anyplace.

Dana: Well, my day has been all worked out. Bob and I have plans. I'll be happy to take you with us to the eleven o'clock if you want.

Mother: You certainly have changed! You are getting impertinent as you get older. You used to be such a nice girl who did whatever I asked of you.

If this is the kind of response Dana received from her mother in the present day, it is safe to assume that the kind of interaction that occurred between them has not substantially changed in fifty years. Even with Dana as an adult who more easily was able to define herself when she got that kind of response, there is a very clear message from her mother that she regarded her as nothing more than a chattel whose existence revolved around taking care of her every need in an absolute way so that Dana had to subordinate herself to her mother or else not be a loving child. If this was the case with Dana as an adult, how overwhelming and guilt ridden must the vulnerable and malleable child, Dana, have been when she received the same kind of response from her mother in history?

The impact of Dana's relationship with her Internal Mother was complex, but undeniably the most obvious and debilitating effect of this ongoing internal involvement was Dana's self-crippling dependency. "If you want to be noticed, don't grow up. Stay needy; stay a child," was the internal mother's implied message. As a consequence, Dana was forever belittling her capacity for independence and self-assertion in her present-day existence.

Delving deeper into Dana's psychic world, we encountered a seemingly insurmountable barrier between Dana and psychological wholeness in the form of her Internal Great-Aunt. Dana's mother had doled out love and attention during the times when Dana was ill or proved herself an industrious household helper, but Auntie was much worse than parsimonious in her expressions of approval and love for Dana. As a girl, Dana had been painfully accustomed to the impossibility of making a favorable impression on Auntie. As an adult, Auntie's unmistakable message had landed Dana with a painful thud at the rock bottom of a psychological well. "Dana, you are just no good. You can't do anything right, and you cheat to get attention because you know you don't deserve it." Dana's internal assimilation of Auntie's opinion of her revealed itself one session when Dana said: "For instance, getting to your office today . . . I was very late . . . so I said I would have to take a taxi. Then I said to myself, 'You have no right to spend that money. That's a lot of money.'"

Auntie's acclamation of Dana's young sister as the paradigm of little girls instilled in Dana an unending hope that through copying her sister she could attain Auntie's favor. Already we can see that the internal implications of Auntie's message would at times conflict with the one Dana received from her Internal Mother. Her Internal Mother told her, "Stay little, stay needy"; and Auntie advised, "Don't be yourself, be like your sister." Together the two messages constituted a complex response with one clear-cut factor: whether she tried being needy, or being like her sister, or both, *any assertion of her own identity made her helplessly vulnerable to criticism.*

The degree to which one struggles to fulfill internal demands is not in response to the identity of the internal authority as much as it is to the severity of its deprecation. Dana's family lived in her great aunt's boarding house for a little over a year; several years later Auntie came to live with Dana's family in their own home, but it was during that first year that Auntie established herself in Dana's impressionable psyche as a far more virulent critic than either her mother or father. Throughout the following years Auntie repeatedly sought employment that temporarily removed her physical presence from the house, but for Dana the continuous psychological ramifications of Auntie's abuse never abated.

What caused Auntie's unfavorable opinion of Dana to become so inextricably embedded in the child's psyche? We are able to pinpoint an answer when we consider Dana's understandably hurt and puzzled reaction to her mother's infrequent expressions of devotion. "Why do I have to be sick or look after the younger kids to make Mommy like me?" the young girl probably wondered. Unsurprisingly, Auntie's pronouncement loomed up as the only apparent answer. "You are just no good, you're lazy. You lie and cheat to get attention you don't deserve. You think too much of yourself"—that's why Mommy is interested in you so infrequently. The weak bond between mother and daughter provided the basis from which Auntie's assertions could assume a position of validity and power in Dana's young mind. The only way for Dana to remedy this untenable situation was to become like her sister, whom Auntie held in high esteem. If Dana were like her sister, she would no doubt achieve Auntie's respect and also her mother's love. Dana's internalization of this message initiated a lifelong struggle to become, literally, someone else.

A corollary of this need to be "perfect" like her sister emerged in session one day. Verbalizing some of Auntie's internal commands, Dana said, "She keeps saying, 'You've got to do it on your own. You don't need this help.'" To be really perfect, she must be strong, independent, invincible. When Dana did feel strengthened by a sense of self-reliance, she tried to seize Auntie's favor by refusing to acknowledge any human feeling at all, her own or others'! She could not feel anxiety, fear, doubt, or anger; her sudden self-sufficiency left no room for warmth or intimacy with others. The needs to be kissed or held were denied. Dana cut herself off from her husband both emotionally and sexually. This overcompensation was guaranteed to finally please her nemesis aunt. But Dana was soon the object of the same game of tug-of-war that gripped her each morning. To whom would she listen, Auntie or Mother? Inevitably Dana was landed in the province of dependency. Mother's opposing assertion, dependency equals lovability, made it only a matter of time before Dana could no longer maintain her valiant but tenuous grasp on "adulthood." She relapsed into illness, sending a cycle of dependency-detachment-dependency one more time around.

Dana's father apparently was not around much during her early years, so he did not have an initial role in stunting her young ego. When he finally settled down with his family, however, his frequent denigration of his eldest daughter's intelligence underlined the sense of worthlessness that Auntie had already taught her. In her father's opinion, Dana's stupidity would always stand between her and intellectual achievement; it was this harsh prognostication that penetrated Dana's psyche in the image of her father.

One session Dana talked about an opportunity she had had to converse in French, a language she had been studying for several years. She had discovered how easily she was able to maintain a flow of dialogue with a woman whose native language was French. The woman had even commented on Dana's proficiency.

Dana: Then I thought to myself, "Oh, I don't know anything."
Jack: Who was it that put that thought in your head?
Dana: My father. He said, "You can study, you can study away, but you'll never learn anything."

Another's admiration of Dana's language skills was not enough to boost Dana's lack of conviction in her intellectual capacity. The only person Dana could hear was her Internal Father.

In another session Dana and I had this exchange:

Dana: Today I made a decision to take a cab. I can imagine myself, maybe a few weeks ago, asking Bob, "Should I take a cab?" and waiting for him to answer "Yes." Of course, he would say yes, because that's the way he is. I always waited for him to give me approval to do something when I really didn't need it.
Jack: You don't need anyone else's approval.
Dana: Not really. But in some cases, when it comes down to "Should I or shouldn't I?" I feel that I do need somebody else's approval. It had gotten so that I didn't want to make a decision because I didn't want to be wrong.
Jack: So that your Internal Father wouldn't punish you.
Dana: I think so, yes. I didn't want to be wrong, so if I asked someone else to make a decision for me, I'd be in the clear.

The Internal Father's message to Dana was that she should always be right; her judgment had to be infallibly sound. An error in decision-making on Dana's part brought about her father's unqualified censure: "You are no good!" As a child, Dana was not allowed to grow through trial and error; she had to get the right answer the first time around. She spent an enormous amount of energy, therefore, on making the "right" choice, doing the "right" thing, proving herself above reproach. To make a mistake became the sin of sins. Since she was unable to maintain this standard, Dana abdicated from decision-making altogether. If she didn't make a decision, she thought, she couldn't be blamed for making a mistake, and thereby she'd be "in the clear."

But this tactic of avoidance backfired at the onset of Auntie's internal decree: "You must be independent." Then guilt overwhelmed Dana in the form of Auntie's subsequent denunciations: "You're lazy, a demanding little child!" Her demoralizing diatribe only served to aggravate Dana's need to be dependent because it further blocked any realization of her inner worth and strength.

To express or even feel anger was another explicit taboo. One session Dana tried to articulate the anger she had been experiencing toward the Inner Others, especially Auntie and Father. Despite my encouragement, Dana was having a very difficult time expressing her resentment about what was happening to her towards them:

Dana: If I weren't so embarrassed. . . .
Jack: What are you embarrassed about?
Dana: I can't get over the embarrassment. . . .
Jack: What do you mean by embarrassment?
Dana: I'm embarrassed in front of you! I know I shouldn't be. . . .
Jack: But what do you mean by "embarrassment"?
Dana: I'm not acting my age.

Dana was definitely speaking under Auntie's influence here. If Dana showed anger, it only reinforced her inability to meet the standard of "ladylike" behavior set by her in reference to her younger sister. But Mother also had a decisive role in establishing guilt as a corollary of anger. We saw that in the present Dana's mother had continued to needle Dana when Dana would not comply with her wishes. Dana's previously made plans had prevented her from taking her mother to church *when her mother wanted to go.* Because she did not comply, Dana was cast into the role of the "impertinent" child. As a child, Dana was lovable when she did as her mother asked; any resistance to her mother's wishes because she might have had a need that was inconsistent with those wishes made her worse than disobedient—it made her worthless. To dare to express anger at being labeled such an unsatisfactory human being because she *attempted* to get something for herself, demonstrated the Internal Mother's denunciation even further. Throughout her childhood and into adulthood, Dana worked tirelessly to refrain not only from expressing anger but from experiencing it as well.

The Parental Powers—Threats and Punishment

These internalized others can and do exercise a great amount of power over the subject. This power radically alters who the subject is to itself and the world. The question arises, then, "What is the nature of this power these Inner Others hold over the subject? What are the threats they use to keep the subject in line so that it conforms to the demands and superiority of the Inner Others?"

Conflicts arise between parent and child when the boundaries as defined by one clash with the other's. Clashes between persons are normal. It is not the conflict per se that gives rise to the self-displacement in deference to the overly powerful Inner Other(s), but the way in which the parent defined and handled the conflict. Problems would arise if the more powerful other exercised power and control over the child when the child properly should have taken responsibility for itself in a given circumstance; or if the Important Other bullied the child, rather than working with it and showing it how compromises are worked out, how understandings and agreements are come to.

The result is that the child, and ultimately the adult, because of the internalization process, experiences itself as hemmed in on all sides by mountains of do's-don'ts; oughts-ought-nots; shoulds-shouldn'ts. If it dares to consider crossing over the admonitions or prohibitions or in fact does so; the internalized voices attack with a set of threat-punishments that exercise a tremendous amount of negative, restraining power on the subject that is debilitating and destructive to it.

In the course of my work I have found four basic threat-punishments that are aroused when the now-adult asserts activity or values that were prohibited by the Important Others during that individual's childhood. The threat-punishments were incorporated by the subject during the vulnerable childhood time. The old scenario of threat-punishments reactivates whenever the now-adult subject considers an activity or assertion of a value that may conflict with the Important Other value. The person, then, rather than seeing itself in a present-day (existential) problem-solving situation, finds itself up against a higher, inner authority with whom it must struggle and contend for power. The result is that most real-life situations appear to be ones surrounded by conditions of threats and punishments.

The first of these relates to a child's experience of being (physically) overwhelmed by the Important Other (by being hit, beaten, strangled, etc.) when there was a conflict between it and child. A patient of mine who came from an upper middle-class family reported that as a child she had been frequently beaten by her father in a vicious, sadistic way whenever there was some apparent transgression on her part. As a result, whenever she could not predict another's expectation and opinion of her, she heard loud, rushing sounds inside her head akin to those she had experienced during the beatings.

In the frightening, rushing sounds she was already being punished by the physically overwhelming father image for not "knowing" what the other (he) wanted even before it was said. This conforms to the memory of her traumatic childhood because, for her, another major element was not only in the beatings themselves but how they happened—namely, her frequently not knowing *why* she was being beaten. The rushing, then, was in response not only to her fright about the beatings themselves but also to the massive confusion about the reason for them. The result was that, as an adult, she became panic-stricken whenever she was unsure of, or could not predict, the opinions and expectations others had of her. She coped with this by fleeing interpersonal situations or staying out of them altogether, mainly by holing herself up in libraries. When the loneliness became unbearable, she would tentatively venture out, only to flee back to the safety of her aloneness when she experienced the onslaught of the rushing sounds. Even in my office, she sat in a position from which she could see both the door directly and the reflection of the window indirectly on the surface of a glass door. She was thus assured of an avenue of escape if I should attack her. She found herself in a perpetual cycle of fleeing the apparent outside attack, "dying" of the loneliness, returning to make contact only to experience being overwhelmed and fleeing once again.

The second threat/punishment that can be incorporated by the child is the Important Other's verbally overwhelming the child if it should transgress in any way. A parent who flies into a rage at some minor infraction or even for no reason at all and screams at the child can provoke within the child a bewildering array of feelings that include confusion, anxiety, guilt, and worthlessness. A woman with whom I worked recalled that her mother could scream at her in a seemingly endless barrage for failing in any way to fulfill her daily duties or for simply not behaving in a "proper" manner. The result was that, when she was around others now as an adult, she experienced herself as a "child"—that is, someone who was small, weak, insignificant, and vulnerable before the Other. This included her husband, me, and members of the group she was in. When we explored these kinds of reactions, she discovered in part an internalized image of a red-faced, snarling woman who towered over her while hurling charges and epithets from within. It was that visual and verbal image—really an internal event—that was projected onto the external world of persons. It happened whenever she thought she was not living up to some expectation of the other person. But the demands she heard were from inside her own head: if she didn't live up to the expectations of others, she would be subjected to the verbal barrage and suffer terrible feelings of weakness, confusion, anxiety, guilt, and worthlessness. Once, however, she became aware that the expectation, the red-faced image, and her own guilt-fear reactions were totally internal to her, she began to question their origin and change her response to them.

A third modality of threat/punishment is one of blame-guilt. In this system, the Important Other communicates to the child that the child is in some way responsible for something that is properly the other's responsibility. For instance, "If it weren't for you children, I would have left your father/mother years ago" (implying "I suffered because of you, and because I did, you owe me something"). Obviously, that parent's choices are the parent's choices, and the child cannot be made responsible for them.

Another woman related how her mother would fly into unprovoked rages in which she would both verbally and physically attack her daughter. The verbal attacks would mostly consist of, "You never do anything I want, you are sadistic, just like your father, and you only like him. You never liked me. You're just a selfish child. You're the one who makes me be depressed and act this way!" The daughter developed an inner parental voice that blamed her for anything that either went wrong or even might go wrong. At times in the group she had joined, she often related how, when two people had a disagreement in the group and she was an onlooker, she thought she was to blame and felt guilty about the disagreement between the other two people! When we came to explore what was happening inside her, her mother-voice became apparent to her. As a result she was able to let go of the responsibility for someone else that it laid on her.

Until that process became apparent to her, however, she felt compelled to leap into situations that were properly not her own to resolve. If she didn't, her mother-voice would leap at her with the blame and the punishment of guilt if she couldn't resolve whatever it was the mother-voice said she was responsible for.

Guilt is one of the most powerful feelings experienced by a human being. Very few people I have worked with have not been overwhelmed by it. The feeling, however, does not "just happen." It is in response to some event. Psychological guilt (as opposed to real guilt—the feeling response to an event in which the subject has deliberately violated another) springs out of the internal charge that a violation has occurred when, in fact, it hasn't. Because the inner charge is thought to be true (because the original authority of the judge—the more powerful Important Other—was and still is incontestable), the feeling of guilt that is generated is incontestable and unresolvable. The guilt by itself is a negative feeling; it is unpleasant by definition. Its very purpose is to bring the human organism to an awareness that it is jeopardizing its social context if it continues to act in the way it is acting, i.e., it faces social ostracism and maybe even the loss of others if it continues the violation. But when we add the apparent irresolvability of the *psychological* state of guilt, the feeling experience can be overwhelming for the subject. To ward off this complex of feelings, the subject who finds itself up against these kinds of internal charges will do almost anything to avoid them.

The fourth threat/punishment that the powerful Other (either external or internal) can hold over the head of the subject is that of the loss of the love of it as the Important Other, either through the rejection or abandonment of the subject: "If you do (are) . . . I will not love you (I will abandon you)." One of the most common issues around which this threat revolves is the child's anger states. Often a parent cannot cope with the child's anger because of its own internalized prohibitions against anger—because it feels helpless and is paralyzed by the anger of another. The parent reacts to the anger of the child through the power of its parental position by threatening to take away its love of the child by either rejecting the child or abandoning it.

A very definite example of the rejection of the child whenever anger was expressed by him came with the following series of events in the history of a male patient, Jon. In the course of attempting to work out an adult-adult relationship with his mother, he had repeatedly requested of her that she not speak both for herself and her husband, Jon's father. He thought this to be important because on many occasions when she had done this, he found out that what was said "in common" by her just wasn't true when he consulted his father. Secondly, he found it emotionally confusing for him when his mother did speak for his father, since he rarely had a chance to experience who his father really was, because his mother was in the way.

It came to pass that Jon bought a new home after years of working toward it, and he was very excited about it. He had been in regular contact throughout the negotiation process with both his mother and father who lived at some distance. During the entire process, Jon received very little support and affirmation from his father about the purchase beyond a polite inquiry. Finally the day of settlement arrived, and Jon wrote to his parents of it and invited them to come see the new home. Jon received a letter from his mother about a week later saying that she and his father would like to come and see it. Jon never received any kind of acknowledgment from his father.

Because of the continued pattern of responses (and non-responses), Jon wrote back to his mother expressing his irritation toward her because, again, she had spoken for Jon's father; Jon reiterated why he had difficulty with this behavior. A few days later he received a letter from his mother accusing him of behaving like a "spoilt five-year-old child" because he wanted something "his way." Because this was the way she saw him, "they" would not come to see his long-dreamt-for new home.

Later that summer, he received a postcard from his mother who was visiting his sister in a midwestern state. The mother described "what a good time they were having" visiting the sister. As Jon was recounting this and talking about his experiencing his mother's rejection of him and his resultant deeply rooted feelings of loss, he remembered how, when he was "a bad boy," i.e., angry, his mother would turn away from him and turn toward his sister and praise her for being "so good." He explained how overwhelmed he was in the frustration that kind of event held for him and how powerless he felt. He further remembered how he couldn't do much with his anger and all the other feelings that went along with it, so he tried not "to be angry" or, better yet, not to feel at all.

What had happened to him, then, was that he disowned the anger and the other feelings which had progressively eaten away at his body with successive serious problems (acute chronic colitis, pancreatitis, hepatitis, as well as chronic muscular tension—severe back and neck pain). It took him years to connect the pain in his gut to the feelings of anger, confusion, loss, frustration, disappointment, etc. Once he did, however, the physical symptoms began to subside.

This particular series of events primarily with his mother helped him to realize what his internal mother was doing inside of him. What began to emerge was an awareness of one of his inner mother's voice saying, "Your anger is ugly and unacceptable to me. Because you have anger and it is ugly, *you* are ugly and no good. *And* nobody will like you if they discover how ugly you are, so you had better hide the ugliness (the anger)." Realizing what the internalized voice was saying, he was able to address it with anger. "Shut up! I don't need you anymore and I'm not going to listen to you anymore, because when I do, you destroy me." Being able to acknowledge the real anger he felt toward the inner voice, he was also able to recognize that his external, flesh-and-blood mother of the present was not able or willing to treat him as a whole, integral person. He began to let go of his deep yearning to have her be someone other than who she really was. He began to redirect all that energy that he had used up in listening and responding to both the internal and external mothers—towards others who could and did treat him as a whole, integral, adult person. As he more progressively was able to do this, the tension in both his intestines and muscles began to recede and he began to feel much better.

Jon was not unique in his dissociation from his anger and other powerful feelings. When Important Others forbid the articulation of anger and sometimes even the experience of the feeling itself, other very powerful feelings are churned up—confusion, loss, disappointment, etc., which must in turn be pushed down or depressed, for, if they are not, the child faces further threats of punishment. If this happens repeatedly, the child loses major portions of its ability to feel. The feelings, although not conscious, are energized within the organism only to "pop out" someplace and in some way that confuses and harms both the subject and the object(s) of the feelings that are acted out. My years of practice have offered ample opportunity to observe many people who are literally unable to feel their anger, let alone express it. Jon was one of these.

Another was Michael, a very shy, insecure man of fifty who had been married for a little over twenty years. He came into counseling because he came home one day to find his wife had left him. He was stunned and could not fathom why she had done this. When I talked to his wife, however, she related how, when issues arose between them, the resolution was either accomplished *his* way or, if it didn't move in that direction, he would begin to shout and eventually walk out, only to return later as if nothing had happened.

When I met with the two of them together, I asked him what were the issues in the marriage around which he felt anger. His response was, "What do you mean? I never get angry." When his wife heard his response, she repeated some of the incidents which she had told me earlier. I asked him if he agreed with her description of the events, and he said he did. I then said that it sounded as if he was angry if that is what happened. His response was, "If that's what you mean by anger, I guess I was angry." Knowing him to be a religiously observant man, I asked him if he thought anger to be sinful. He replied very quickly and strongly, "Yes." Because of this erroneous belief, he had come to disown his angry feeling in one of the most radical ways I had ever observed. This resulted in the destruction of his marriage and family, one of the few things he lived for. He had disowned those feelings because he had been taught that the Great Parent, God, would reject him if he felt and acknowledged those forbidden feelings.

To understand how this process happens in childhood, consider an interaction between a father and his son which I witnessed several summers ago. The father and I were sitting in his kitchen talking. As his five-year-old son padded by me in his bare feet, he stubbed his toe against my chair. When he doubled over on the floor in pain and began to cry, his father went to him and held him, trying to comfort him. After several minutes, my acquaintance began to exhibit some increasing anxiety about his son's crying and then said, "Oh, come on now, big boys don't cry." With the statement, the boy stifled his sobs, and shuffled with head down into the other room where he remained for a considerable amount of time quietly whimpering to himself.

Of course, the father meant no harm in his response to the boy. He probably thought that it was his duty to teach his son that it was not manly to cry. Undoubtedly, he had been taught the same as a boy. Beyond that, he was probably as uncomfortable with his son's tears as he would be with his own. But close examination of the father's response reveals a possible effect on the child's developing psyche that is not readily apparent.

First, the child was obviously in pain. Moreover, he was probably angry at the chair. We've all stubbed our toes at one time or another, and the subsequent reaction is often one of wanting to lash out at the object that attacked us when we weren't looking. The child's tears were an expression of these feelings and impulses. But what of the boy's interpretation of his father's response to him? Possibly, the child might have taken his father's words to mean that it is inappropriate to be held and comforted by another person, particularly one's father. Furthermore, the father's verbal response was not supportive of the boy's pain, anger, and tears. If the boy is repeatedly told to stifle his tears and be a "big boy," this interpretation becomes reinforced and culminates in the image of an internal other who says: "Feelings of anger and pain should be repressed as quickly as possible. Your tears are unacceptable. Hold them in. Above all, don't look to another person for comfort. To cry and to be held and comforted are really only childish needs, and if you have them, people will think you are not a man."

A variation of the threat/punishment loss of the Important Other's love is through the abandonment of the child either emotionally or physically. Any child is placed in a dilemma whenever the Important Other deals with the child by maintaining a stony silence when the child meets with its disapproval in any way. The parent's love is withdrawn without warning. Icy indifference fills the vacuum the parent's emotional withdrawal has created. Very often the child does not know exactly what it has done wrong and must guess the nature of the transgression because the parent refuses to communicate it. Moreover, it could be that the parent is emotionally distant in relation to everyone. The child, however, does not possess this objective perspective, and knows only the yearning for contact with the parent. Readily assuming blame for the parent's distance, the child believes that it must somehow find an antidote. An image of the parent is formed within the child's psyche that demands, "If you love me, you should know what I'm thinking, what I'm needing, what I'm feeling." This kind of parental demand extends itself into the provinces of all relationships in an individual's adult life, and this person spends much of the time trying to guess the needs of others while disregarding its own needs.

Ironically, the enormous power of the Inner Other is maintained because individuals readily inflict the threats and punishments of the internal other onto themselves. When Dana did not live up to her Inner Others' expectations of her, she felt terrible guilt; when Chris let people get too close, he punished himself with overwhelming panic.

Wolf in Sheep's Clothing

In all of the previous experiences of the Inner Other, these internal voices have been blatantly attacking and undermining in their activity. This is not always the case, however. Sometimes the Inner Other(s) can present to the subject what appears to be "good advice." If the interaction remains unchallenged as such, the subject can find itself paying a very heavy price for what turns out to be a very subtle but, nevertheless, destructive undermining of the "I." The following is a series of instances involving Dana and one or more of her Inner Other voices and what happened when she explored them.

In this session, Dana talked about a slide presentation she had put together for two groups of people. One group appreciated the humor of the subject of Dana's slide show. The other group did not seem to understand it, however. The fact that the second group was unable to see the wit in Dana's presentation became a source of personal rejection for her. Here she tried to come to grips with the idea that the second group's inability to see the humor was a reflection of the group members' own sensibilities, not a value judgment against Dana.

Dana: Well, I could have said to myself, "You don't have to sit here explaining yourself to anybody."

Jack: What is the significance of that statement?

Dana: I think . . . uh . . . that because these people didn't accept my slide show as humorous they were judging my value. [Pause.] I was projecting onto them what my inner father was telling me.

Jack: Why don't you replace the "you's" with "I's" in that sentence and see what happens? "Well, I could have said to myself, 'I don't have to sit here explaining myself to anybody.'"

Dana: OK—Well, I could have said to myself, "I don't have to sit here explaining myself to anybody."

Jack: Now repeat it the first way, with the "you's."

Dana: Well, I could have said to myself, "You don't have to sit here explaining yourself to anybody."

Jack: Is there any difference with what happens inside of you when you use "I" versus when you use "you"?

Dana: Yes, definitely.

Jack: What's the difference?

Dana: First off, when I use the "I," I feel like it's *me* who's speaking.

Jack: What happens with the "you"?

Dana: It's distant, not me speaking.

Jack: What's the feeling tone in both ways?

Dana: Well, when I use the "I," I feel strong about it—connected. When the "you" comes out, it's like somebody else telling me and I feel weak and incompetent, like I need someone else to tell me things; I can't function on my own.

Jack: There's something else I'd like to point out here also. I think what's going on here is that you're making my value system, or what you anticipate my value system to be, into a parental proposition. No matter how you slice it, it never becomes your own value system. It's another person's value system. Hmm?

Dana: In other words, I'm switching to the Internal Parent. . . .

Jack: You're making me into the Internal Parent.

Dana: I'm making you into my father, and still not developing myself. That's like always asking somebody else what to do.

As Dana realized the significance of what she said, it became apparent that her life was still being directed by that Inner Other and not by herself. Even though it appeared to be a benign suggestion from that inner persona, *she* was still disappearing in the process of its interjection. Further, in our interaction and relationship, she was very subtly and unconsciously being set up by the internal others to make me into another of her judges—exactly what she had done earlier in her relationship with Bob. This interaction between Dana and me was far less complicated, though, than Dana's interaction with Bob, because we caught the subversion in the beginning, before the internal parents could get out of hand between us. If we hadn't done that, what had happened between Dana and Bob could have happened between the two of us.

Another aspect of this "Sheep" is that it set Dana up to not operate out of her own insight about herself and the world. Instead the Inner Other gave her permission, rather than allowing her to operate on her own initiative. Underlying that, she was being robbed in a very subtle way of her sense of personal worth and value. If this pattern had been allowed to continue, it would have ended in her failure to be able to affirm her own existence in a positive way.

If the picture of the "criticizing judge" had been allowed to continue to be projected onto me, I would gradually have been viewed with distrust, fear, and anger by Dana because I would have become another person in her world who, from her unconscious perception, would have been setting up impossible goals and standards for her to achieve. Eventually she would have experienced guilt in relationship to me because she was not the "perfect" patient.

In another session, what at the surface appeared to be a self-loving statement turned out to be a diminishing and attacking statement by the Inner Other. Dana had been telling about how well things had been going as a result of the insights she'd been having.

Dana: We decided after having worked [on the housework] all day to go out and get ourselves a big steak. That's something I wouldn't normally do. I said to myself, "You worked hard all day, you're worth having a big steak for once!"

Jack: Did you hear yourself?

Dana: Ohhhh.

Jack: What's happening there?

Dana: My Internal Aunt is . . . it's telling me I should feel guilty for spending that much money on myself. "Bug off, because I'm worth it and I can go out and spend money on a dinner if I want to!"

Jack: How do you want to rephrase it now?

Dana: Saturday after I finished cleaning I wanted to treat myself to a good dinner and enjoy it.

Jack: How does it feel saying it that way?

Dana: It feels more connected.

Jack: How did it feel before?

Dana: I was rationalizing the whole situation.
Jack: What was behind the rationalization?
Dana: That I had to . . . uh. . . .
Jack: The feeling behind the rationalization? What's the feeling that prompts the rationalization?
Dana: Guilt. Guilt that I shouldn't be doing this by myself.
Jack: What does that tell you?
Dana: They're still there fighting.

Once again Dana discovered that there was a very subtle undermining of herself by the Inner Other in what seemed to be a very self-affirmative statement by herself; however, the statement was not from her but from her Internal Aunt. The impact of its statement and the "I" statement are a confirmation of this. When she rephrased it as an "I" statement, the tone changed from a sense of guilt and worthlessness that existed underneath the "benign" statement to one of goodness.

Minimally what happens, then, when the Inner Other takes over and speaks for the subject, even with "good advice," is that the subject gets displaced and the "I" identity gets blurred. But on top of that, there is usually a whole complex of feelings (in this case, guilt—the guilt that is aroused within the subject toward the interloper as well as toward itself) that gets masked and covered over. When that happens, the subject unwittingly begins to view the Inner Other as an ally and friend when in fact it remains a betrayer, spy, and enemy.

Because these kinds of explorations have consistently revealed the subject to be endangered and seduced whenever the Inner Other "gives good advice," I have come to respect the deviousness of its internal process and never let it go unaddressed.

6

THE INTERPERSONAL IMPACT

Seeing the Parent All Around

The developing child possesses the ability to internalize the values that the family communicates to it. Matching these internalized values are sets of behavioral patterns that the child designs through trial and error to bring it into conformity with the family's expectations.

The difficulties which Dana, Chris, and many of us experience because of these internalized value systems and the behavioral responses to them do not lie in the *fact* of the internalization but rather in *what* was internalized. For example, earlier I pointed out that there are basically two ways an Important Other can help a child learn to tie its shoes. One Other shows its way of tying the laces to the child and then says, "OK, now you do it." If the child fails to do it exactly the same way or tries to experiment with its own method, the Other demands with varying degrees of harshness that the child immediately tie the laces exactly as shown. Otherwise, the Other judges the child to be a failure and therefore no good.

The other kind of Important Other shows the child how it ties the shoelaces. It then stands by the child and allows it to proceed at its own rate with its own variation on how to tie the laces. Rather than admonish the child for deviating from its norm, *this* Important Other encourages the child to experiment and to find its own way of solving the problem. At the same time, it remains available to the child as a resource but not as an absolute authority on lace-tying. If the child is having a particular problem with one of the skills required, it can turn to the teaching person and ask how to tie the lace. Then the child can apply what it sees to solving its own problem.

What the child internalizes from the first type of interaction is that it must conform to a preordered structure of things as determined by the parental figure. Therefore the child can never let go of the Important Other figure as the ultimate norm and arbiter of its value and perception of things.

The message from the second kind of parenting internalized by the child is that (1) it is not only possible but important to use its own experience in living out its life in the world; (2) it can use the Other as a reference point and depend on the Other to give it that kind of help without taking over and overwhelming it; (3) it can experiment to arrive at its own way of doing things; (4) it is respected by the other when it moves toward autonomy and separateness in its activity; (5) it can discover its own values about itself and the world without having to depend on another for that.

The first kind of child learns, then, to alter its behavior to conform to the expectations of the Other. If, for instance, the Important Other orders the child not to reveal its anger about issues and to do only what it is told to do without regard for its uniqueness as a person, the child will repress and disown its anger by simply shutting up. Given that kind of parenting, shutting up is probably the most adaptive thing the child can do in that environment if it is going to survive physically or emotionally.

Internalizing the values of Important Others and the behavior that flows out of them becomes a problem, however, when they become applied to the world beyond the family. Because the family circle (physically, emotionally, and psychologically) is the only world for the most intensely developmental years of the child's life, the developing person makes the erroneous judgment that the values and expectations of its familial figures are identical with the values and expectations of the world in general. When these very limiting values and expectations taken from very specific persons in a specific environment are universalized to the world in general where they do not apply, that is when they become so restrictive and dysfunctional that they hinder the person from coping with its environment. That is when they assume the label of neurotic. But we must always remember that their origin was in fact born of a need to cope with a difficult situation. Often they were the very behavioral patterns that saved the child from physical or more profound psychological harm than it had already undergone.

It is easy to understand how such a child comes to universalize these early but specific interpersonal experiences. Around the age of six, the child's psychological and social perimeters begin to expand beyond the family circle. At this age the child begins to be psychologically ready to form peer alliances with non-family members as well as some alliances with older persons. In our culture this coincides with the child's first definite separation from the family environment: beginning school. This event gives the child a forum in which it can begin experimenting with peer relationships as well as relationships with older persons outside the family, such as teachers. However, the child is entering those new categories of relationship with the disadvantage of having had (at least psychologically) the experience of interpersonal interaction only with family members, along with a fairly well crystalized internalization of the impact of that limited experience. Because children are so malleable and because the majority of our educational institutions (frequently) mirror the parenting of the first type described above, such a child's first exposure to a world beyond the immediate family experience tends to confirm what it had already experienced and internalized in response to the family. The internal system is not only kept intact but is verified and reinforced by the new experience of the child.

Further, the child's experience of negative parental figures has a much greater impact than the experience of more positive figures. These negative figures are such a threat to the integrity of the child—the child has been forced to gear itself so much in defense—that the internalization of these figures has become primary. If one finds oneself in a besieged city that is in constant danger of collapsing and being overwhelmed by the enemy, it is very difficult to see and appreciate that the sun is shining, the sky is blue, and the birds are singing. The child who experiences a very negative, criticizing, primary parental person finds it very difficult to balance that interpersonal experience with more benign ones. And, once the human organism has geared itself for coping with a negative, interpersonal relationship through the internalization process, it is that image that predominates in power, intensity, and content.

The result is that those who have constructed these kinds of internal familial images are affected not only within the context of their internal thoughts but also in the interpersonal interactions. Because of what these internal object-persons tell them about themselves and the Others who are in relationship with them, these external others become distorted, often in very radical ways. Sometimes this is so extreme that a person or event becomes, in the eyes of the subject, the exact opposite of what actually happened or what the Other intended. The following sessions will demonstrate such distortions.

Dana had recently returned from a week's stay in the hospital as a result of an esophageal collapse. That day, she and Bob had been to the doctor because the symptoms had begun to escalate again. She arrived at the session very distraught, barely covering over her anger toward Bob because of his interference with her conversation with the doctor. The irony of it all was that she had set Bob up to tell her what to do and how to do it, and then when he complied she became very angry with him.

On past occasions, Dana would not have put her own questions to the doctor. Instead, she would ask them of Bob when they got home. In order to be prepared with the answers, Bob began to take over in the situation and ask the questions for her. Then, when she would ask him, he would be able to tell her what to do.

By doing this, however, he fell into the trap of becoming Dana's Inner Other. Consequently, he was swept into the dynamics of Dana's intrapsychic relationship; eventually, he became all of Dana's psychic parents. Dana, in defense, related to him through her Angry Child.

Jack: Dana, what did you think was going on at the doctor's office when Bob spoke for you?

Dana: What did I think? I thought he was treating me like a child. [To Bob:] I'm sitting there trying to have a conversation with the doctor, and you keep interrupting with, "Pardon me, pardon me." So you *did* ask all the questions. That's true.

Jack: So Bob, then, became like your inner voices, right?

Dana: Yes.

Jack: Now there's a history to that kind of process, isn't there?

Dana: Of him speaking for me?

Jack: Yes, or to put it another way, of you forcing him into the position of having to play their parts.

Dana: He figured I wouldn't do it. [That is, ask the doctor the same questions she had been asking Bob all weekend.]

Jack: Do you agree with that, Bob? Did you figure she wouldn't do it?

Bob: Yeah.

Jack: I think Dana is beginning to shift and take on more responsibility for her own life. But because of past history, you, Bob, are still assuming that she will operate according to the old Dana. Do you follow me?

Bob: I follow you, yeah.

Jack: Now, how can we begin to deal with Dana's shift? When she brought up the issue of medication—how long ago was that?

Bob: It was Saturday. She had pains. Down here. [He points to his abdominal region. To Dana:] I told you to take the Mylanta.

Dana: I didn't want to take the Bufferin *and* the Mylanta because I was afraid of the side effects.

Bob: I suggested the Bufferin because you had a headache. But that was Sunday, wasn't it?

Dana: [In a very sullen tone of voice.] No, Sunday was fine.

Bob: All right then, it was Saturday. [Pause.] I'm not a doctor. I can't prescribe, but if you have a headache, one of the things that might help you is Bufferin. *Sunday* I suggested the Alderal. That's prescribed once a day for high blood pressure. I don't know if she had high blood pressure yesterday, but she complained of having pains in her chest [the windpipe pain]. I didn't see any harm in her taking the medicine so long as she took it at the prescribed dosage. That's what I told her.

Jack: What's happening, Bob, is that you unwittingly support Dana's need to be emotionally involved with her Internal Father. In other words, Dana wants someone to tell her what to do. But it also seems that when someone does tell her what to do, her anger is aroused. This issue is comparable to the one about Dana taking responsibility for getting to my office by herself. The issue of what pill Dana should take, and for what reasons, is becoming Dana's responsibility. Like today, if she goes to the doctor and doesn't ask the questions she wants answered, she has got to deal with it. If she comes home and has to ask you about which medications she should take, your answer should be "I'm not your doctor. Why didn't you ask him?" Do you follow the logic of what I'm saying?

Dana: I have to be responsible for my own decisions.

Jack: Yes.

Bob: Well, if other people have answers for her, she shouldn't bother me with her questions if it's not my place to give answers.

Jack: That's right. That's exactly what I'm saying. You don't really have the answers, but it appears as though you do.

Bob: Well, in the absence of a doctor who is readily available. . . .

Jack: Dana's just as intelligent as you are.

Bob: No question about that.

Jack: I think it's really Dana's responsibility to ask her own questions. What has the session opened up for you?

Dana: It's let me see that I do place Bob in a position to make decisions for me, and that's why I get angry with him.

Jack: Is there anything else?

Dana: I don't like him telling me what to do, treating me like a child—and then sometimes I do. I can see that. And he ends up having to take the brunt of my anger.

Jack: Is there anything else?

Dana: I realize that I must make decisions for myself.

It is important to note that Dana had a real reason to be angry with Bob about their session together with the doctor that morning. Bob's taking over the session by speaking for her, interrupting what she wanted to say, and not consulting with her, were definite intrusions in *her* session. Dana's response to Bob's intrusion and her resultant anger are very typical of a person who has chosen the hysterical compromise as a way of dealing with the psychological dilemma: to be in relationship means to give up self-identity. Dana gave up her identity to Bob at the very outset.

One of the major reasons why the person who has adopted the hysterical mode of working out the psychological squeeze so assiduously avoids accepting responsibility for its part in the interpersonal interaction is that it is attempting to avoid the attack by the Inner Other. The indecision and the giving over of responsibility for the Self to another are really anesthetics to the pain of the guilt.

There were some other very important ramifications to Dana's encouraging, promoting, and allowing Bob's takeover. Bob's behavior at the doctor's office *was* intrusive. His activity, however, was not parental of itself; it was simply Bob's way of coping and acting in that situation. His activity in relation to Dana became parental for her because of what it meant in light of her history and the content of her Inner Other images.

As *she* entered into relationship with Bob in this event, which was meaningful to her, the relationship was characterized by a profound passivity. A great deal of the problem for Dana was that this constellation of feelings and way of relating was not a one-time happening. Rather, these feelings transcended this interaction and characterized Dana's experience of relationships in general. The image she had of herself was to be the child, but a particular kind of child; i.e., one who was weak, passive, submissive, inadequate, wrong, and worthless before the all-powerful, all-important, all-knowing, all-right Other. Given the assumptions of her Inner Others and all that is generated out of them, it is easy to understand how life had become a dead end for Dana and why she had reached a point at which she was choking herself to death with the collapse of her esophagus.

This session was a turning point for her because, for the first time, she began to see in this concrete relational context with Bob that she didn't have to buy the assumptions she had. There was another way of responding to Bob's intrusive behavior. There *was* an alternative!

Clouding Over

Given the intensity of the pain and conflict Dana had been experiencing in this previous interchange with Bob, it is much easier to see why a person like Chris would opt for the schizoid position. He experienced contact with the Other as so ridden with difficulty that he concluded it would be better if he didn't get involved in relationship at all. Following are excerpts from consecutive group sessions in which Chris, bit by bit, gets in touch with the process by which he had been in a state of isolation from the members of the group because of that historical, psychological conclusion and decision. As that realization became more profound, it helped him to see that what was happening in group was precisely what was happening in his attempt at relationships in general.

The content of these sessions revolved around Chris's emotional involvement with a violent prison riot that he had read about in the newspapers in the West. In this first excerpt, Chris had just revealed that he had been absent from the group for three weeks because he had been emotionally overwhelmed by the riot itself. Part of the reason he got caught up in it was that he had befriended a prisoner there with whom he had been corresponding. When he heard of the riot on the news, a concern for his "friend" was precipitated, which rapidly turned into a deep depression, immobilization, and isolation. He did not reveal that in this first session, however. In the course of this first session he explained that his reasons for not coming for the three weeks had been based on the immobilization that had resulted from his emotional involvement. More importantly, however, he did not think that we would be interested in his emotional predicament, or understand what was happening to him. In response to what Chris finally decided to reveal to us about this event, Dana shared with him how she was often tempted to believe similar things about the group. When she started to notice that she was having those kinds of thoughts, she realized that they were an indication that her Inner Others were getting in the way and separating her from real contact with the individuals in the group. She concluded her response to him by relating the impact on her of what he has told her and the others:

Dana: I would have felt sad if you wouldn't have been able to share with us this very powerful event for you. But now that you have been able to do that, I feel happy for you that you've been able to break through that. [Silence from Chris. He remains in a slouched position in his chair, hardly looking at Dana.]

Jack: What does it mean to you to hear Dana say that to you, Chris?

Chris: Thank you. And us, that us, two things, that uh she felt. . . .

Jack: Why don't you say it to her?

Chris: Oh, I'm sorry about that. I heard you say that you felt bad, sad, that I made that choice to stay away and not to seek your consolation and help.

Jack: So what is the significance of that to you? What does that tell you about Dana in relationship to you?

Chris: That you care. [Very quietly] Thank you.

Jack: Is there anything else? She said something else, didn't she?

Chris: You also said that you were glad that I was able to share.

Jack: What does that mean to you?

Chris: Further caring. Thank you. [With a little more substance to his voice] I appreciate that.

Jack: So it is possible to get beyond your bitch [one of the names Chris gave to his Internal Mother]. What are you feeling right now—having heard Dana?

Chris: Relaxed and joyful.

Jack: What were you feeling just before I asked you those questions? Dana had said those things to you. What were you feeling as a result of those things?

Chris: Mmmmm. Maybe I was drawing a blank.

Jack: Maybe?

Chris: Yeah, I think I was kind of numb.

Jack: OK, so why was that happening? Why were you numb? What did my questions do? You had an emotional reaction to Dana because I asked you some questions which were relaxed and joyful. So, what did my questions do?

Chris: They put me in touch with my real feelings.

Jack: Yeah, but there was a prior event. You felt because something happened.

Chris: I was able to listen, to hear.

Jack: And incorporate, take-in emotionally what Dana was saying to you, I think.

Chris: Yeah. Yeah.

Jack: If I had just asked you what Dana had said, I'm sure you would have been able to say, and in fact you did repeat what she had said. But I didn't just do that. I asked you what the significance of what Dana had said to you was. If I hadn't done that, you would have continued to feel numb, blank, emotionless, not having incorporated emotionally what Dana had said; therefore, you would have remained isolated. Now, why did that process happen?

Chris: The bitch was trying to keep me isolated.

Jack: How?

Chris: By, uh, not letting me hear it.

Jack: How was she accomplishing that?

Chris: By not allowing me to incorporate what was happening.

Jack: How was she preventing that—taking in the good stuff?

Chris: I think by not allowing me to expect good.

Jack: How was she articulating that inside of you?

Chris: I think she was saying that I don't deserve good.

Jack: What do you want to say to that?

Chris: [Pause.] Lying bitch!

Chris had developed a formidable armor to prevent himself from entering into relationship with anyone or letting anyone engage him. The result had been a profound loneliness which drove him into therapy to find some relief from the pain of that loneliness. Even as he tries to leave the castle of his isolation, the thick walls of that castle are very apparent.

By realizing the emotional blankness he experienced when he was caringly addressed by the Other, Chris was able to see that his perception had been radically distorted. He was then able to integrate the real interpersonal event involving Dana, and not the one dictated by his Internal Mother. Once he was able to do that, he was able to get in touch with the internal event that distorted his experience of the external world and address that as a separate experience. The original emotional blandness and numbness dissipated into relaxation and joyfulness in relation to Dana and into anger toward his Internal Mother for the distortion of external reality and the resultant numbness and blandness.

A week later, another member of the group, Art, related to Chris how he had missed Chris because he had related so much to the kinds of conflicts Chris talked about, in addition to the fact that he liked Chris as a person. Again, there was a very similar response by Chris to Art's comments. And again I asked Chris what it meant to him to hear what Art had to say to him.

Chris: I'm surprised, in a way, that you remembered me—of my having spoken.

Jack: What surprises you about that?

Chris: I ordinarily don't think I make an impression on others.
Jack: But you did. Art said so.
Chris: I want to get comfortable with that feeling.
Jack: So therefore you are uncomfortable with something? What is the feeling that you are trying to feel comfortable with?
Chris: I don't want to feel surprised by it.
Jack: But what is the feeling that you are trying to feel comfortable with?
Chris: Uh, the thought that I make an impression.
Jack: OK, so you are surprised by that thought. What's the surprise.
Chris: That Art took notice of me, or paid attention.
Jack: OK, so why does that surprise you?
Chris: That's that fuckin' bitch!!!
Jack: So what's she doing?
Chris: She's always telling me that I'm nothin'!!! "And I learned to listen to you, bitch!!" Oh, wow! I want to share with you something that I told someone this week. My mother said to me one time, [snarlingly] "*You* a teacher? How could you teach anybody anything?" [With some wonderment and disbelief in his voice] She snarled it at me. When I told him that, I cried, I broke down and cried. I cried also because I was so used to being put down by that *bitch.* At the time she said it, I said "Aaaa," I almost assented, agreed. "Yeah, that's right. [With resignation] She's right again." I wasn't aware that I had any feelings, that I was even hurt by it, because she had worked so hard on me that—uh—I had come to expect it. As in this case I had expected a negative reaction, if any at all.
Jack: If I hadn't asked you the question I did, what would have happened to the event between you and Art?
Chris: I would have lost it forever.
Jack: Exactly. Is it now getting clearer to you why you have so much difficulty relating to people in a positive kind of way?
Chris: I thought of that tonight. If I don't experience anything positive, why would I want to go back?
Jack: That's right.
Chris: I was tempted not to come tonight. But then I thought, "But I had such a good feeling at the end of last week's session, so I'm going back and maybe by some miracle it will happen again." [He laughs.]
Jack: Yeah! Wonderful!
Chris: And so I came back.

Jack: That is the best reason in the world for you to come here.
Chris: I feel very relaxed with that thought.

Again it emerged that his Internal Mother had blocked the positive response from Art by telling him he was unimportant. He did not make an impression on others; that is, he really didn't exist for others.

The following week, Chris finally revealed that he had been writing one of the prisoners in the riot-torn penitentiary. Not only had he been writing this man but had responded to the man's "pleas" for money to help him get settled after he was released from prison which, according to him, would be soon. The fact of the matter is that Chris was embezzled out of nearly a thousand dollars by this man. The con had promised Chris friendship when he was released if Chris helped him financially. The reality was that this was a racket that this man had run from the prison and had tried it before on other persons.

The different members of the group, including myself, raised the question as to why he hadn't discussed these events much earlier since this all had gone on for six months or more. He related how, as a result of the con, he now felt devastated and betrayed by this man and the whole experience. I then responded to Chris by contrasting this stranger to Chris's actual experience of the members of the group.

Jack: Chris, how long have you been coming here?
Chris: About two years, now.
Jack: Now you've had two years of a steady experience. How long have you been in contact with this man?
Chris: About six months.
Jack: OK. So what you are saying is that you believe more in a person with whom you do not have a primary experience, that is, someone you have never met and who in fact resides at a considerable distance from you and because he is in prison is guaranteed to be there in that condition for a while. Therefore, what you are saying is that you place that experience above the weekly, intense experience you have of us here. I wonder why your experience of us does not register with you but the vague promises and interchange with this man does register. Even here today if I hadn't asked you what was the significance of different persons' responses to you here today

and last week, you would not have been aware of a feeling response within you at all.

Chris: My feelings are kinda, uh, uh . . . I don't respond to people—you in the group—in a receiving kind of way.

Jack: Now something has happened here tonight. I have responded to you, as have Dana, Nancy, Mary, and others. What's happening inside with all of that? What happened with what Nancy just shared with you about her difficulty and struggle that she has with allowing people to get close to her?

Chris: [Long silence.] I didn't receive it in a feeling kind of way.

Jack: What does it mean to you that Nancy, first of all, was addressing you and, secondly, what was the significance of the content of what she was saying to you? Where's your Child in this?

Chris: [Long pause.] My Child is right here [points to his lap].

Jack: Did you hear what Nancy said?

Chris: [Long pause.] In a way I don't want to be touched.

Jack: OK, why don't you want to be touched?

Chris: Oh, it's a struggle, a struggle between not wanting to and wanting to.

Jack: What is the struggle?

Chris: My Child knows that if I feel touched, my Child tells me that I will come out of my loneliness.

Jack: So that's the one side, the side that wants to be touched and knows what will happen if you are touched. What about the other side, the side that doesn't want to be touched?

Chris: [Yells.] That's not me!! That's the evil bitch! . . . Even when I think and feel that my Child wants to be touched then in a sense I feel touched. Then I think that even looking at each of us is, uh, giving me support. I think even in that way it's making contact, because I want to.

[I get up and place the life-size dummy in front of him to help him visualize physically how he has been psychologically separated from us by his Internal Mother.]

Jack: Can you see everyone in the group?

Chris: No [very subdued].

Jack: Why not?

Chris: She's blocking me.

Jack: And what is she saying to you? What was she saying to you as Nancy was speaking to you?

Chris: "You're a prisoner." That's what she says.

Jack: That's right. Do you feel like a prisoner right now with her hovering over you like that, crowding you in?

Chris: Yeah.

Jack: How do you feel about that? How do you feel about being crowded in, blocked out, surrounded, dominated?

Chris: [Yells.] My Child wants out!! [Gets up, punches, knocks over and kicks the dummy.] "You bitch!"

Jack: Do you want out?

Chris: "I am my Child, you bitch!"

Jack: It's important, then, when you hear anyone responding to you in a positive kind of way that you examine to see whether you are taking that in; unless you do that, you will remain separated and alone from others.

Chris: The bitch tells me, "Regardless of what happens, unreasonable as it sounds, they'll all go back to their respective lives, and I'll be alone again. So what is the use." It's an all or nothing. If this person cannot be for me all the time then there's nothing.

Jack: Therefore, if there's autonomy, there cannot be love. There can only be love if there is fusion with the other person. There can be no separateness.

Chris: That's exactly right. I connect fusion and this expression of oneness, "You shall be as one." Then nothing else has any importance for me. Everything else is a drudge by comparison. There is nothing else that has any worth then. Nothing else matters, my job, other relationships, nothing.

Jack: No wonder you want to relate at a distance. No wonder you find it difficult to relate to us who are close to you. You are afraid that we will take you over. Then we will make demands on you that you don't want made but because you are compelled to give yourself over to the other person. You will have no choice and then you will disappear. Therefore it is safer if you can find someone with whom you can relate at a distance, then the danger isn't so imminent. In the case with the prisoner, the only thing you lost was some money. With us, given what your Internal Mother says to you, you will lose your soul.

The following is an excerpt from another group session many weeks later. Chris was describing how he had taken the tape home from the previous session and how much difficulty he had listening to it. In that session, he was talking about how lonely he was in his life. The group listened intently to him, asked him questions and were generally concerned and sympathetic to his plight. Suddenly, he asked a general question of the group which seemed to come from nowhere. It changed the flow of what had been happening and drew the attention of the group away from him. I asked him about it. He replied that he had been becoming uncomfortable with doing all the talking. We discovered that he felt guilty about "taking up all the time" and he was afraid the group was bored by his narrative. After he had realized what happened in group he narrated it to me, individually:

Chris: I dreaded listening to the tape from group. It upset me each time I listened to it.

Jack: Tell me about that.

Chris: Well, uh, once I'd heard it . . . I actually realized . . . realized that . . . I said to myself, "That's not *me* talking." It was almost like a person possessed. [Said in a whisper.] I said, "That's my Mother talking." Realizing that was as if a light had come on. And although you had, in essence, said the same thing, I hadn't experienced it, I hadn't known it, until I listened to the tape, calmly and objectively. I was in such a state of guilt in group, it was as if she was there pounding me over the head until I sunk into the chair! [Chris had literally sunk into the far corner of the sofa as he talked to the group.]

Jack: Are you beginning to understand what I'm getting at when I say you are really alone with your Mother?

Chris: Yeah. It was as if I wasn't really here. It was as if all of you were talking different languages. I couldn't understand you or anybody. Which is also what happens, Jack, what happens in social situations. It's as if she's always hitting me over the head, saying, "What the hell are you doing here? These are not *your peers*. You're nothing. You're garbage."

Jack: "Stick around me. I'm your mother. I know you're garbage, but I'll take care of you."

Chris: Yeah . . . that's the other side of it. She understands and she'll accept me anyway. She'll take care of me. Which is a laugh. I took care of *her*.

Jack: And in return you get her company. Right?

Chris: Yeah. Sure.

Jack: It was better for you to have her put-downs than to have nothing at all from her.

Chris: Yeah.

Jack: From your vantage point you lose everything when you lose her. That's the nature of the relationship. So you'd better hang on to the put-downs. And because your internal relationship with your mother is so intrusive and binding, you experienced the group as not being here with you, or you not being here with us, when we last met. She takes over and you lose contact with us. But we *are* here. So if you lose her you *don't* lose everything. You can afford to give her up.

The challenge that was now before him was a question: who was he going to choose to listen to, his Internal Mother's propaganda that he heard loudly and clearly from inside his head, or the evidence of his experience of us responding to him as someone of worth and value? The more able he was to "see" that the internal voice was lying to him in general as well as in specific interpersonal events, the more able he would be to challenge her, integrate the response of the others and respond to that himself, and the more able he would be to resolve his interpersonal isolation and the deep, clutching loneliness. But at the same time though, he had to give up his yearning to have the maternal image accept him within her bosom.

Part IV

THE CHILD

7

THE PRESENCE OF THE CHILD-WITHIN

The History

Thus far, we have spent a great deal of effort trying to understand the Inner Other: how it is formed; its function; how and when it becomes dysfunctional; its activity; and how it can take over and render the subject immobile, depressed, anxious, empty, isolated, valueless, guilty, and lonely. Although it is an expremely important mechanism within the psychic apparatus and process, it is actually quite peripheral to the process of psychological healing.

The Inner Other is only a psychological wedge that serves to split the total Self apart. If one removes the wedge and the split remains and the Self is in fractured segments, true healing cannot take place. As long as the conscious, central "I" remains separated from the "Child-I," it can only function in that fashion, as one who is cut apart, divided, dis-integrated. True healing of the Self can only take place when this dis-integration becomes integration, wholeness, oneness with Self.

The process by which the Inner Other image is internalized and the "I" is divided up into parts makes it easy to understand why it is possible to overlook and forget the existence of the "Child-I" and its importance in the resolution of the psychic conflict.

In the past, the developing child came to believe that parts of itself were not acceptable to its Important Others. These aspects of itself threatened its existence. It was driven to use its developing psychological capacity to dissociate from, disown, and hide these parts of itself. It further accomplished this task because of the aid of the simultaneously developing ability to image internally the values, demands, and physical picture of the external Important Others it experienced, and this ability acted as a watchdog against the appearance and activity of these "dangerous" parts of itself. It must be stressed again that the perception the child develops of important, more powerful Others is composed of a rather complex interplay of factors. There are real messages from these figures as to what they find acceptable and unacceptable. There are the punishments and rewards they will give out if the child does or does not conform to expectations. There is the consistency of the Important Others in establishing the ground rules, the *way* they do this, and the child's tendency to interpret their behavior (for example, silence) as a punishment when it is not meant that way. And there is the child's radical pyschological dependence on these figures, which results in the exaggeration of their response.

The developing child possessed two very powerful psychological tools which developed simultaneously: the internalized Other to warn it of the transgressing Self, and the ability to disown the transgressing Self. Both, however, were merely tools to gain, from the perspective of the vulnerable child, the safety of the approval and the avoidance of punishment by the Important Others. All of this was organized around the belief that the unacceptable parts of the Self that manifested themselves more topically in behavior, and more integrally in attitudes and feeling states were *the* problem. The primary goal, then, in putting these two very powerful psychological tools to use was to disown every aspect of the Self whose manifestation of existence could, as perceived by the child, endanger the existence of the rest of the Self.

So thorough was this belief that, to the child, it was even better if it could hide these "dangerous" and "undesirable" aspects of itself from itself. If it could achieve that, it could delude itself into believing they weren't even there. If they weren't there, the child could then believe itself to be in an even safer position in relationship to the external Important Others. The success the child had at disowning these undesirable aspects of itself depended very much on the strength and tenacity of its internal watchdog against these parts of the Self it believed it couldn't afford to have around. The developmental purpose of the Inner Other was only to act as a watchdog. The ultimate and overall purpose and goal of the entire process was the disintegration and separation of the Self into acceptable and unacceptable parts as defined by the Important Others. The former were allowed and encouraged to be visible; the latter were hidden, at least from others, and if possible from the Self.

The great majority of the people I've worked with were good at establishing the powerful watchdog function of the Inner Other and achieving the radical denial of the existence of the unacceptable parts of the Self. Unfortunately for us, we attained these psychological objectives with great success. The irony of it all is, however, that the degree of success we had in achieving these goals in childhood, thereby coping and surviving as well as we did in childhood, is precisely what robs us of life, now, in adulthood.

As adults, whenever these deeply buried parts of the Self either threaten to erupt into conscious reality or in fact momentarily do (for example, feeling angry or, worse, behaving angrily), the watchdog "barks" with, "How dare you! If you let that out and take over, you will be very sorry because 'people' won't like you. Then you'll be sorry!" This is all the Central "I" needs to hear and *does* hear; the unacceptable, "dangerous" part is pushed back into its psychic prison before its existence is even consciously available to the Central "I." By definition, then, the "Child-I" is to be unavailable to the awareness and functioning of the Self.

What *is* more available to the Central "I" at this point is the "barking" of the watchdog. Because the noise of the "barking" is so loud, it is difficult for the subject to acknowledge that there is deeper, more profound and integral reality that lies beneath all the noise. Therefore the acknowledgment, confrontation, and even the disowning of the Other values and prohibitions does not of and by itself bring about a healing of the Self. Just because the Central "I" acknowledges the activity of the *Inner* Other and confronts it, does not mean that it acknowledges the reality of the disowned parts of itself. Sometimes the Central "I" is so engrossed in screaming back at the Inner Other, that it cannot see that there is a deeper reality beyond its argument with the Inner Other, namely the "Child-I."

At best, the acknowledgment, confrontation, and disowning of the Other images creates a psychological vacuum that is the *beginning* of the reversal of the original, developmental, psychological process. If this is only as far as the subject takes itself in the healing process, and if active reclamation of itself does not happen, there is only an empty psychological space that is created by the absence of the Inner Other. This is not a very reassuring state for the subject to be in, for a variety of reasons.

During the developmental time of childhood, the act of disowning parts of the Self created a psychological vacuum that made it possible for a psychological space to be available into which the other image could be accommodated. The encapsulated parts of the Self were disowned and the developing Central "I" fashioned the separate prison in which this disowned part of itself began to take on its own identity and autonomy from it as the "Child-I." The psychological space the "Child-I" rightfully held and from which it had been disinherited by the Central "I" became available and it was occupied by the Other image as soon as it became available through the disowning process.

To accomplish the disowning, the prison was located as deep in the recesses of the psyche as possible—the more out of sight, the more out of mind. Further, to make sure the "Child-I" remained in exile, the watchdog needed to be granted a power that would keep the "enemy" part of the Self in exile. The result was that the Inner Other, with its beliefs and value systems, was very much in control of the Self.

These beliefs and values became the Central "I's" source of identity. Thus, when many people began (as Dana did) to understand the real significance of the "you" address as not being the manifestation of the Self but as the manifestation of an Inner Other, they became very panicked at the idea. So much authority had been given over to this watchdog that the thought of giving it up appeared to them as though they were giving up their very identity, life itself. Without the beliefs and values of the Inner Other telling the Central "I" who it was, the subject saw itself to be aimless, powerless, and bereft of any sense of identity. The "Child-I" who was the real source of identity and power had been vigorously pushed away from the Central "I." The "Child-I" had been so thoroughly covered up by the loud and vocal prohibitions of the Inner Other that it was unavailable to the Central "I." Thus the Central "I" would be unable to gain the sense of power and identity the "Child-I" possessed until it rediscovered its existence and importance.

Naming the Child

My initial insight into the internal dialogue came when I heard the verbal juxtaposition of the "I" and "you" in conversations with patients. It did not take me long to realize the psychological entity that addressed the "I" as a "you" was something that was really there speaking to the "I" as another. Therefore, it had to be something other than the "I," something that had an existence all its own. When the persons with whom I was working came to this same realization, they were able to change the nature of the dialogue they had been engaging in all along. The resolution of the psychological conflict strengthened as they vented their anger on this internal person rather than on themselves or external others.

However, this movement toward resolution of the psychological conflicts was relatively shortlived. Many of the people with whom I was working seemed to have reached another stalemate. One day, however, as I was listening to Chris in a session, I began to sense that there was something else going on in the conversation than just a dialogue between Chris and his internal mother. That evening, I listened to the tape of the session again. As I listened I heard a tone in Chris's voice that did not correspond to what I was used to hearing from the "I" of Chris nor from his internal mother. It sounded very weak and vulnerable, very much like a child would when it was overwhelmed by some event or person. It was then that it dawned on me that there might be another psychic person present in the internal interchange that we hadn't yet recognized or acknowledged. I began to review the professional literature. There was a group of primarily British psychoanalysts, referred to as object relationists, who had proposed that the child has the ability to split off parts of itself as a way of coping with the apparently irresolvable demands of its Important Others. They merely regarded this as a way to refer to a psychological process and not as an existent, dynamic, psychic persona. When I reread this material, I concluded that what I was hearing from Chris and, by this time, from others, was the manifestation of the third person of the psyche, the "Child-Within." As the importance of this hidden, occasionally manifest but elusive part of the "I" began to dawn on me, I had to give it a name. I chose to give it the name of "Child" for a variety of reasons.

My spontaneous, intuitive response as I listened to this part of Chris (and now others) was to call it "Child" because it sounded like a child—weak, vulnerable, full of childlike fear, who made its presence known through pouting or angry rebelling. When I pointed out to Chris, Dana, and others what I was hearing, they agreed that they heard and experienced this other, third part; they, too, gave it the name "Child." They felt very much at ease with the name.

As we began to explore this inner part of themselves and I asked them to visualize it, the images that came to them were of themselves as children at various ages of development. The most common age range of these images fell between five and nine, although some people (as we shall see later) pictured this buried part of the Self as an infant or sometimes as fifteen to sixteen years old.

I realized that this part of the Self had been split off and disowned and, although it had been shunted deep into the darkness of the unconscious by the Central "I," it was very much alive and active in the intrapsychic dialogue that took place between the Inner Other, the Central "I," and itself. Realizing that, I helped Chris, Dana, and others to talk openly with this part of themselves as I had suggested when the Inner Other manifested itself as a psychic entity. Although it was a difficult undertaking, very consistent patterns emerged. Those patterns were assumptions about reality that are consistent with the state of being a child.

When they consciously entered into dialogue with this part of themselves, it manifested itself to be very weak, vulnerable, and at the mercy of the Other. The Other was perceived to possess absolute power over it; the Other held in its hands the power of life and death. The Other's power to accept or reject the subject, to love or abandon it, was the power of life and death over the subject. Because the Inner Other was "arranged" in such a way within the psyche, the experience of the external world of events and persons was by and large blocked from this part of the "I." Frequently, the only experience it had access to was the experience of the Inner Other, what it told this "Child-I" about reality or what it would allow the "Child-I" to see. The result was that this part of the "I" could only perceive itself as the child it had in fact been in childhood: weak, vulnerable, and radically dependent on the Other for its physical and psychological survival. Therefore, whenever it saw itself threatened in these terms, it reacted to the event as a child would—from the position of weakness, vulnerability, and radical dependency.

Calling this part of the "I" the "Child" made a great deal of sense. Chris, Dana, and others began to openly interact with this part of themselves, relating to it as a child by responding to this part of the "I" as one vulnerable before an infinitely more powerful world of Others. This was accomplished by mentally holding and reassuring it. This brought about a sense of resolution to the psychic conflict that, heretofore, had never happened. The "Child-Within" was the name of the greatest meaning I could give to this encapsulated part of the "I."

The following is such a conscious interaction and dialogue between Dana and her Little Girl. Contained within this dialogue is the complexity of the three-sided conversation between Dana and her Child, between Dana and her Inner Other, and between the Inner Other and the Child. Dana had broken the pattern of isolation and immobilization, had gone to lunch with a group of women friends, and had enjoyed herself. In the session, however, she was becoming aware again of the apathetic "part of myself." When I heard her use the phrase "part of myself," that meant literally to me a part of herself was speaking of which she was not entirely aware. Suspecting this was a clue to the activity of her Child, I asked:

Jack: Where is your Little Girl?
Dana: Sitting here.
Jack: What kind of expression does she have on her face?
Dana: She's looking down. She's not looking up at me.

Jack: What does that mean?

Dana: She doesn't know if I want her around. "Hello, Little Girl." [Pause.] I feel silly doing this.

Jack: Ask her if she enjoyed lunch.

Dana: "Did you enjoy lunch today, with everybody there?" [Pause.]

Jack: What did she say?

Dana: Yes, because she liked being a part of people. She felt good. She felt wanted.

Jack: By whom?

Dana: By me and the rest of them.

Jack: So you can tell her, "See, I did that for both of us. I went to lunch for both of us." Can you tell her that?

Dana: "I went to lunch for the two of us, not just for me. Wherever I go, you can go, and enjoy yourself."

Jack: And also tell her, when they tried to get in the way, see how well I did?

Dana: "Did you notice that I almost said 'no' when they tried to interfere, but instead I said 'yes.' We could go."

Jack: And you had a good time.

Dana: Um hmm.

Jack: What's her response to that?

Dana: "Why don't we do these things more often?" [Pause.] This is very hard.

Jack: In what way is this hard?

Dana: I feel strange . . . talking to this side of me.

Jack: You feel more comfortable talking to the other side of you, the Inner Other?

Dana: Yes, because then I can yell and scream. This side brings a feeling of calm and instant love—the opposite of what I feel.

Jack: This is very important. You are zeroing in on the fact that you feel more comfortable in a relationship of anger rather than one of warmth, caring, peace, and love.

Dana: Self-deprecation.

Jack: That's right, the Other put-down. And you forfeit the spontaneous, loving feelings when you engage them.

Dana: Gives me worth.

Jack: The experience which gives you a sense of worth, exactly.

Dana: But these feelings should make me more comfortable. I'm uncomfortable now.

Jack: Yes, I think because they are trying to get you to disown this Little Girl as they got you to do as a child. But you heard your Little Girl's response. She liked being a part of people. She felt good. She felt wanted. And she will talk with you if you talk with her.

Dana: She becomes obstinate, too, when she doesn't feel that I'm on her side. She balks at everything. "I don't want to do this." It's not because *I* wouldn't like to do it.

Jack: Remember you told me that you once left your daughter for a period of time, and when you came back she was angry at you for leaving? Could you get her to do anything?

Dana: No, she was mad.

Jack: Exactly. She was obstinate as hell until the two of you came to a resolution. You have to do the same thing with the Little Girl inside you. She is going to continue to balk until you convince her that you want her.

Although Dana faced strong resistance from her Internal Father, Mother, and Aunt there is a great deal of difference between the content of this session and the one recounted in Chapter 1. In both, there is a very intense interaction between the Inner Others, the Central "I" and the Child. However, there is a very radical change in the nature of the dialogue between the personae in this session. Unlike that other session, in which Dana was unaware that these personae were engaging her, with the result that she became a passive, immobilized spectator, she had come to acknowledge both the Inner Others and the Child and take an active role in engaging them.

Bringing that resistance out into the open, she was beginning to challenge the assumptions on which the resistance was based. Because she chose not to go along with the Inner Others this time, she found out some very important things about this inner person that had been so unavailable to her for so long.

It was not sufficient for Dana to push aside her Inner Others by doing what she wanted—to go out to lunch with a group of friends. That was an important step, but not the final, resolving step in the healing process. Although she was able to address, confront, and move against the wedger, the split within her own "I" remained unaddressed and intact. It took another series of steps in her interaction with her Child to bring about the final resolution and healing to this intrapsychic process.

Even as Dana was trying to re-establish contact with this forgotten and unfamiliar part of herself, the Inner-Other voices were working hard to get Dana to disown this "bad" part of herself by telling her she was silly if she persisted in this conversation with it. But as she progressively betrayed the admonitions of these voices by insisting on talking with her Child, she discovered the gulf that existed within her own being. As she continued to talk with the Child, the gulf narrowed when she understood why the Child was doing and feeling what it was. As her understanding broadened, she was able to respond with understanding, caring, and warmth to this sad, apathetic girl where before the response was anger and confusion.

As she continued in this vein, the Child and she became less and less estranged from each other—until the Other voices broke in again. The importance of reclaiming that aspect of herself became increasingly clear to her. With that came the contrast of the negative effect the Inner Other voices had on her and how much they worked at keeping her separate from the Child: "This side brings a feeling of calm and instant love . . . worth. The opposite of what I feel (when the parental voices are in operation)."

The final outcome for Dana in this experience was the discovery that, if she is to feel whole and integrated, she must actively seek out this shy, fearful, apathetic part of herself. Once she affirmed the existence of the Child by actively seeking it out and then by talking with it openly, she was able to respond to the Child as a friend who had needs that were to be met, and Dana could meet them.

With the discovery of the Child as an integral part of herself, the reclaiming of it was the beginning of Dana's refilling of the void she had created as a child to accommodate the Other voices. The sense of inner emptiness which flowed out of the propaganda of those voices and which proclaimed her radical worthlessness as a person was now filled by its proper occupant, the disowned "I," the Child, the receptacle of her life-force. Without it, she was robbed of much of her energy and involvement in living because much of the source of the energy for life was imprisoned within that disowned part of herself.

Dana discovered that the Child was very much involved in the joy of life, wanting to enjoy and be with people. If she lost that part of herself, she discovered that she lost much of what was stimulating and alive in her. If she was able to reclaim that part of herself, affirm it, and aggressively satisfy those needs, she found herself coming alive, psychologically and emotionally.

The same result occurs when we disown any part of the "I" that gives or preserves life. For instance, when a child is taught to disown its anger either in its articulation or the feeling, the child is being taught to stand defenseless before the world. To understand the full significance of this, it is important to understand what a feeling like anger is and how it works.

Anger can be defined as the emotional reaction to a perception on the part of the subject (self) that there is some threat (personal or impersonal) to its welfare that it must defend itself against. Now if a child is taught that it does not have the right (1) to say what the threat is, (2) to prepare itself for danger, or (3) to acknowledge the possibility that danger is there, then that human organism is exceedingly and inappropriately vulnerable to its environment. Further, with this innate, protective mechanism curtailed, the life-force behind that mechanism is blocked. So, not only is that person blocked from defending itself from the possibility of danger, but it is also blocked from the life-force behind that defense. So, if the child finds itself in a position of disowning sociability, anger, spontaneity, playfulness, creativity (as Dana did), not only does the person lose access to these capabilities but the person loses access to the life-force that is behind them. Therefore, the more aspects of the Self the person is constrained to disown, the greater will be the deadening effect on the total organism. Since these aspects of the Self reside in the "Child-I," not only are the capabilities reclaimed when the Central "I" reclaims the Child, but so also is the life-force behind them.

The Children as States of Being

Earlier I noted the example of the little boy who stubbed his toe against the leg of the chair I was sitting in. As the boy walked away by himself after his father had commented on "big boys" and "tears," there was a strong possibility that, as he was walking away, he was in the process of disowning the parts of himself that he heard his father finding unacceptable, namely "tears," anger, pain, etc. In Dana we can see the end product of this disowning process and the feeling states of being she had come to disown.

The following is the portion of a session in which Dana had been talking about how she had become aware of how her Inner Others had interfered with her picking up and commenting to a friend on her friend's use of "you" instead of "I." The "I" part of Dana thought it would be helpful for her friend to be alerted to the significance of this and to share with the friend her own discoveries around that kind of event. She was prevented from doing so because in the "back of her mind," she heard at a preconscious level from her parental voices that she would merely be imitating me (Jack) and in so doing she wouldn't be genuine. As we talked in the session this undercurrent became revealed and I asked her:

Jack: What do you want to say to that?
Dana: I'm putting myself down.
Jack: The Inner Others are putting you down.
Dana: They are doing it. "Bug out! I can learn new ways of behaving! New ways of acting! It's none of your damn business! It's my choice. *I* want to do it. . . . I don't want your pains either." [She puts a hand on top of her head.] I've felt like a headache has been coming on since the beginning of last week. It's the pressure of acknowledging them again. "But I don't want you here! I don't want you anywhere!"
Jack: Where is the Child at this point?
Dana: It's almost as if she has her hands over her ears at this point. She doesn't want to hear the battle. She's afraid of hearing the angry voices.
Jack: I think that is the reason for your headache. How can you reassure the Child? How can you touch her? By disconnecting her from them.
Dana: By turning away from them. [To her psychic Child] "The anger is not directed at you; it's directed at them. I can be angry with them—the anger is just."
Jack: Maybe it would be helpful to point out to her what they just did. What was the impact?

Dana: "They started interfering with my values."
Jack: Our values. [Hers and her internal Child's]
Dana: "Our values. They wanted to start to think for us, to take out their feelings on us. And I started to get a headache. We don't need them to think for us. We can tell them now that we don't need them to do that for us. You don't have to be afraid to hear that."
Jack: What is her response?
Dana: She's calming down.
Jack: Perhaps it's also important that you hold her. Does she want to be held?
Dana: Yes. [Pause.]
Jack: Tell me what's happening.
Dana: She wants to hold on to me. Be reassured. "It's all right."
Jack: Are you holding on to her?
Dana: [Very quietly] Yes . . . I'm relaxed. . . . The feeling of pressure is gone.

As soon as Dana moved to claim the anger she had toward her Internal Parents for their meddling in her life, they engaged the Fearful Child, who believed that if the anger was left in open view, then Dana as a whole was in danger. The headache was the manifestation of the conflict of this Fearful Child. From the conversation that ensued with this part of herself, it became clear that this part viewed the anger that Dana was expressing as aimed at her. This fear is resolved when Dana reassures the Fearful Child that the anger is not aimed at her but at the meddling of the others. With this, Dana and her Child move toward resolution when Dana mentally "holds" the Child. By being in conscious contact with this heretofore separated part, Dana is able to show her that anger can be a positive, resolving process that can bring about freedom and peace and not destruction if it is properly addressed.

What, then, emerged as a result of this interchange was the appearance of layers of dissociated "I's." The angry "Child-I" had been more accessible to Dana, was more able to reunite with her as Central "I" in this interchange. The reuniting of this part of herself with herself was accomplished fairly easily. With the continuance of the headache, however, was an indication there was something beyond the Angry Child. As Dana and I went on to explore the significance of the headache, the Fearful Child revealed itself.

To understand and respond to any of the encapsulated "I's," it is often necessary to explore the history that lay behind their formation. I then proceeded to question Dana as to the source of the Fearful Child. Memories of verbally violent arguments between her father and great aunt began to emerge. They more often ended when her father stormed out and stayed away from the home for awhile. There were other memories that were similar, which, however, involved her father and mother. They, too, would have verbal flare-ups. On one of these occasions, there was a showdown between her mother and father about the issue of living with the aunt. Her father did not want to move out. Her mother did. They reached a shouting impasse. Her mother stormed out this time, taking Dana and her sister with her. Her mother found a new place to live, and the family was separated from the father for several weeks. Dana explained how very frightened and confused she was by this course of events. The fright and confusion existed at two levels.

The first level was what was most directly observable to her in these various interactions—if there was anger, somebody important disappeared. For a four- or five-year-old child, it is not a large leap of logic to understand this kind of angry event as meaning that anger means the loss and abandonment of the Important Other. As Dana spoke, she realized that this is what the angry event had come to mean to her.

The second level of meaning the angry event had taken on for Dana as a child and that she therefore carried with her into adulthood was her belief that *she* was always responsible for the anger of the Other as well as the abandonment and loss of the Other as a result of the angry event. Even though the anger was not even being directed at her, she found it difficult to separate the effect from the cause. Because she did not have anyone in her family who could and did help her differentiate (a proper function of good parenting), she came into adulthood believing she was responsible for any and all anger, hers, someone else's, whether it was directed at her or not. But why would she so disown the fright around the anger into a separate "I" entity?

The angry "I" had to be disowned because it was dangerous. The fear too had to be disowned because it was dangerous, but for different reasons. *Her* anger was dangerous because, if it was revealed, she faced the verbal disapproval and reprimand of her various parenting figures. The angry event between others aroused a state of fear that she experienced as being overwhelming, in which she experienced no way toward resolution. Because the adults themselves could not work constructively with their anger, there was no one there to explain to her what happened; to reassure her that Daddy was not lost or had not abandoned her and to comfort her about her fears and sense of loss. Rather, she was left to herself and her own devices, namely her own imagination and fantasy. Left with that, she was helplessly ensnared, entrapped in an overwhelming situation from which she saw no exit. In that, she felt overwhelming weakness and vulnerability to circumstances of anger. The result was that she came to equate the angry event as an event in which she would be personally "wiped out" by the angry person. The angry event was then associated with a whole complex of feelings: fear, helplessness, vulnerability, and weakness. In this context, feelings had no outlet for resolution. She had one of two psychological choices at this juncture, either consciously to endure that kind of terrible pain or to anesthetize herself against the pain by dissociating from it. She chose to dissociate from it for the obvious reason that she could not possibly endure that kind of irresolvable pain for very long. It worked "temporarily" merely because she experienced relief from the intensity of the pain.

However, dissociating from the fearful part of herself did not dissolve the fear and everything that went along with it, i.e., the powerlessness, vulnerability, and weakness. Quite to the contrary, the fear became encapsulated within her and, in the encapsulation, it became untouchable and unresolvable. She had disowned her anger *per se* not only because she had been taught that it was naughty, no-good, something a proper lady doesn't exhibit, but also because of the overwhelmingly painful fear she had come to associate with the angry event, regardless of *who* was angry.

Not only did that Angry Child have to work against prohibiting Inner Other figures, but it also had to work against this separate part of itself who feared the effects of the anger. The result was that different aspects of Dana were working against each other, because of erroneous assumptions. Once Dana discovered that these two apparently disparate parts of herself existed, she was able to open up in dialogue between them and effect a modern-day reconciliation.

The result of all this was that I came to acknowledge and deeply appreciate that not only can we construct more than one internalized Other, but we can also split off more than one encapsulated "I," each of which then takes on a separate, disparate existence. In this case, Dana had split off two feeling states that became separately encapsulated.

This splitting off does not end with feeling states, however; sometimes an event or grouping of events and experiences that represent a traumatic time for the child is encapsulated. It seems that persons, like Dana, who had organized their coping mechanisms around the hysterical compromise, tend to disown feeling states. Those who are more oriented to the schizoid position dissociate and repress a traumatic time and often one that includes an infant. A relatively isolated woman, Peg, related the following fantasy:

Peg: I had trouble falling off to sleep the other night. I was very restless. Then I thought about what you had said about the Child. So I tried to get in touch with that. I felt very . . . I felt the Child was crying. I felt I would touch that Child. Not just touch with my hand but with my being. I felt close. I really felt identified with the feeling the Child must feel. I tried to . . . to recall, like you said, . . . uhmm, the Child needs caring, caring for, reaching out to. And that's what I said, "I will care for you." I held that Child and then I turned over and went to sleep. . . . That Child was very small. . . . She didn't seem to be any more than four months old. . . . Just lying there in her crib with her eyes open.

Jack: What were her surroundings?

Peg: She's just lying there very still. . . . I think she was . . . my mother used to have this cradle looking out towards the sky and she worked around the kitchen. It was always there, close to the door, you could see the sky [her voice gets very soft] through the door.

Jack: There doesn't seem to be anybody else around.

Peg: Oh, absolutely. Oh, I know. Sometimes my mind wandered in there. I was just aware of that Child looking for someone, someone who wasn't there. It seems as though I must have spent my whole infancy and young years waiting and watching.

Another woman, also very isolated, described in session a similar mental image. This woman had had a very passive mother, but a very domineering grandmother who apparently could be very sadistic toward her. As we were talking about a memory that seemed to stir up some deep-seated feelings, I suggested she close her eyes and picture her Child. As she did this, she had a mental picture of herself as an infant and her grandmother slapping her while she was nursing the bottle:

Bess: I'm trying to picture her doing that act to me. I can see her slapping me. And of course not coming near me after I scream and cry for a long time. That's what I told you once, I used to cry for a long time. So I couldn't breathe hardly, begging for someone to come. Fucking bitch! Absolutely crying my heart out. The impossibility of love from her anyhow. From my mother and that whole crew. So fucking sad. But that was then and this is now and I really don't give a shit about it. I don't want to care anymore about them. I want to loosen up all those fucking bonds. . . .

Jack: What about the Child? Where is she?

Bess: I never saw that Child. And I just saw her now when I was picturing my grandmother.

Jack: Is she screaming?

Bess: I know what I'm going to do. I'm going to go and take it . . . up. Take me up. Take that baby up and hold it and cuddle it. "It's OK. You didn't mean it. You're a baby. You're a good baby. And I love you. Now let's just sit here and rock. . . ." [Long silence.] She seems to be getting bigger as I'm rocking her. Like she's growing up instantly. She keeps not fitting on my lap! . . . But she was smaller. . . . She's stopped being a baby . . . I can't make her a baby any more.

Jack: Does that mean to you that she's grown up?

Bess: That she's not a baby any more.

Jack: Umhm. She finally got what she needed.
Bess: She got unstuck. It's like being stuck. . . . It's very strange. It happened so quickly. It was never one of my Children from before that I ever saw. I had to go find that one. That was a deeper part.

When traumatic events or times are split off, disowned and repressed like Peg's and Bess's were, they remain festering wounds underneath the psychological skin. Though, at times, to look at that wound can be frightening and overwhelming, looking at it can bring about a deep sense of resolution. Claiming back these parts of the Self is very important for within them resides life itself.

8

CONTINUED DISOWNING AND SPLITTING

The Prison

To assist us in our socializing tasks, we have an innate, psycho-biological capacity to create an Inner Other image to assist us in establishing our outer boundaries in relation to those around us. At the same time, we need to make psychological room for that incorporated, admonishing, and prohibiting image, by splitting off and disowning aspects of ourselves that jeopardize conformity to these parentally established boundaries. The way in which the Central "I" continues its relationship with the encapsulated parts of itself is reflective of the dilemmas it faced as a child and how it navigated itself through them by adopting either the hysterical or schizoid compromise. The "choice" of direction is not entirely up to the child, but seems to be somewhat dependent on how early in the child's life the conflict or deprivation took place and some other environmental factors.

The dilemma, no matter what final posture a subject takes, is that the Other requires me to give up my identity, who I am, and become what that person wants me to become. "If I don't conform to that order of things, I will lose my connections with that person. I either give up who I am, thereby preserving the connection with the Other, or I give up the connection with the Other, thereby preserving who I am. No matter which option I take, I lose something that is very valuable to me and my psychological survival. If I choose to preserve the relationship with the Other, I give up some of my self-awareness, with the result that I must then wrestle with the inner void of emptiness, valuelessness, and powerlessness this imposes on me. On the other hand, if I choose to preserve my identity, I then lose the life-giving stimulation of interpersonal exchanges, and I face a death threat in the isolation and loneliness that ensues."

Dana chose the hysterical compromise— she chose to give up her identity rather than the implicit or explicit demands and conditions the all-important Others laid upon her. As a result of this, she ended up encapsulating and disowning major chunks of her identity and self-awareness. To accomplish this, she created a "prison" within her psyche in which she hid those forbidden parts of herself, from both herself and external and internal Others. Keeping the "Child-I" out of sight deluded Dana into thinking that her psychological survival was ensured by being more readily acceptable to the all-important Others who were the source of her identity. By achieving, in her mind at least, the acceptance and approval of the Others by conforming to their demands and expectations of her, she also claimed some degree of vicarious sense of worth and identity in the Others' approval and acceptance of her.

The enormous pain of the loss of self-identity broke through the doors of the inner realms of her unconscious. The Child would break loose from her inner prison. She would make herself known through obstinate refusals to the Inner Others' demamds, illness that warded off their attacks, or begging for their "mercy," as was manifested in the first interchange with Dana in Chapter 1.

At times like these, the "Child-I" was reacting to a real death threat that was being caused and precipitated by the internal dynamics. The enormity of the situation expanded as the loss of energy available to Dana as Central "I" diminished. This further created a rapidly expanding black blot of void that occurred when she increasingly disowned herself and her own powers. This, in turn, precipitated a loss of power to keep the doors to the prison of her Child closed and locked. At that point, the Child, as a total Self, would burst forth in a usually short, desperate, and intense attempt to recoup for Dana some aspects of identity and inner sense of power by the refusal to comply or gain attention through the sickness. This did happen in a very contorted and convoluted way as we have discovered in her interactions with Bob, her husband.

Ironically, when she had regained some sense of identity and some sense of self-power, this in turn would arouse the attack and condemnation by the Internal Father, Mother, and Aunt. Self-power and energy gained in the Child's eruption would be quickly turned around and used against the Child to re-establish the original order of things. However, when she stopped to listen to this part of herself, a profound sense of wholeness and peace came over her. She stopped allowing her Inner Others to repress and punish her inner Child.

Chris found another way to cope with the same dilemma that faced Dana. Rather than capitulating to his Others and thereby disappearing as Dana had, he refused to give himself over to the Other. He maintained his inner sense of identity, self-awareness, and power. The price he paid, however, was the loss of the Other, with the resultant pain of loneliness and isolation. As a way of coping with the problem, Chris, like Dana, created a prison for his Child, but his purpose for the prison was different from Dana's. The prison was a castle, a place where this center of his life could reside, protected from the onslaughts of the world of Others. The following is a description of that castle:

> Chris: I can see two parts of me. [He closes his eyes and holds up his right forearm with the fist clenched.] The one here is dark. All I can see are two figures—heads. They are grotesque, like ceremonial masks. Their teeth are bared. The heads are dark. The other part is on the other side. [He moves his left forearm and fist facing the other fist.] It is facing them off. They're at a stalemate. The left side is like the Little Boy in me. Both of these figures are outside of me. I can feel the struggle is outside of me now. It's like it's out there in my arms. My upset stomach has gone and I'm not tense like I was when I got here this morning. And I'm sitting here watching this going on. But watching this, that is the real center of me. It is *me*. It's like what happened in group a couple of sessions ago. Now I can see that no matter what anybody said, I was going to defy them. As I told you then, it was like I was watching myself go through this whole ridiculous thing. Now I can see what was happening. That part of me [indicating his left arm], the Little Boy, the little boy my father told me about two years ago who would just stare him down, was sitting in my lap, defying everyone, no matter what they said. The rest of

> the group, you and the others, had become, I guess, that other part, my Internal Parents, I guess. I had the same feeling toward you then as I do today with these images. It feels good having them outside of me. I feel like *I* can be in control now. I don't have to be at the mercy of that battle that's been going on inside of me all the time. It's good knowing what the issue is now. It makes sense to be able to talk to these Parents and tell them to get the hell out. That's just what I've done and really feel good and in control, like never before.

He had constructed an inner world in which the other is seen as a very dangerous enemy. The battle was waged with siege tactics. The Child stayed within the security of his inner castle, beleaguered and besieged by the Other. *All* events with Others were seen from this position and, as Chris described his interaction with me and the members of our group, we, too, were viewed this way. We were his enemies, to be defied and kept out.

The Child in the meantime remained isolated from the world and therefore bore the enormous pain of the loneliness. Because these conflicts were all buried in the unconscious, the undefinable pain is what ultimately drove Chris into therapy in hopes that it might reveal the source, the nature and cause of the pain. This session began to reveal to him the reality of that isolated Child that he had forgotten about. His task was now to dismantle the fortress in which he found the Child by ridding himself of the threat, his Internal Mother, and in turn, to discover that the rest of the world was not his enemy either.

Since the Inner Other shares the same psychological "space" of the psyche as the Central "I" and "Child-I," there is an internal intimacy that must be coped with. Therefore, the developing child finds that it is much more difficult to hide the internal events from the internal personae that have ready access to those internal events. The Central "I" finds itself in a position of expending an enormous amount of energy trying to keep those unacceptable endangered parts of itself under wraps. Part of its technique in accomplishing that task is to wipe the realities of these parts of itself from its own consciousness. Because that happens, it becomes very difficult for the Central "I" to be aware of the significance of the struggle because it has lost touch with one of the major participants, the Child.

As both Dana and Chris began to grasp the reality of these inner children within them, they began to experience an opening to the resolution to their inner conflict. As we shall see, continued movement toward resolution will lie in their continuing to reclaim their children as well as letting go of their Inner Other images.

The Central "I" - "Child-I" Relationship

There comes to be an intense relationship between the Central "I" and the "Child-I" that has some very definite characteristics and patterns. Not only does the Central "I" take a position in relation to the Child, but the Child also takes one in relation to the Central "I." Within any one person there is usually a combination of ways in which the Central "I" and Child relate to each other.

The first of these positions is one in which the Central "I" disowns the Child and regards it as an enemy.

Dana: I feel so alone. I keep battling them.

Jack: But your Internal Father, Mother, and Aunt are not the only ones involved here, are they? What about the Child? How do you relate to her?

Dana: I'm not concentrating on her. [She chokes and coughs.]

Jack: Yes. And I think I know the reason why.

Dana: Because I'll lose *them.*

Jack: Yes, I think that is very true.

Dana: She seems to be wandering.

Jack: Tell me about that.

Dana: That's me wandering. [Pause.] She doesn't seem to have anything to call her own.

Jack: Perhaps because she's been disowned.

Dana: She's crying for help all the time. The girl is crying out for help and the one closest to her—me—doesn't respond.

Jack: The questions is, what do you want to do about that? About her?

Dana: Tell her that she's worthy.

Jack: Worthy of what and whom?

Dana: Worthy of herself.

Jack: Who else? [Pause.] Have you ever thought of you?

Dana: Of me? Does she have to be worthy of me?

Jack: Yes. Right now she's split off from you.
Dana: That's right.
Jack: The two of you must come together again.
Dana: That's right. To become . . . uh . . .
Jack: One. She really is a part of you.
Dana: Instead of being here . . . [Dana points away from herself] she should be . . . [Dana points directly to herself].
Jack: That's right!

Dana had continued to disown the Child because she still very much feared losing the company of the Inner Others. Because she had depended so thoroughly on their voices to guide her through life, she came to believe that her course would be aimless without their direction. Having forgotten about the original breaking off from herself and being unable to recognize and claim the Child back, that part of her ended up wandering and directionless *because* Dana and she were not connected. Because, at some deep level, Dana was connected to the wandering aimlessness, she was aware of its discomfort. Because of what the Other voices said to her, she thought the aimlessness (apathy) was a function of not conforming to the Inner Other demands. The more she disowned the Child, the more aimless the Child became. Because the Child was a very deep part of her own life-force, Dana experienced the aimlessness as well but incorrectly identified its cause.

However, once she started to come to terms with the real cause for the deep sense of aimlessness, namely her own disconnectedness from her inner Child, the avenue for opening up the healing of this rift with herself became available. In this session it was a major discovery on her part that the aimlessness had its reasons and that they were connected to Dana and *not* the failure to conform to the Inner Other values. She was then in a much better position to stop turning to the Inner Other figures as a solution to her pain and misperceptions of reality. As she did this more and more, the difficulties and pain began to be relieved more consistently and definitively. It began to pay off to challenge the Inner Others—as long as she continued to claim her Child within.

A second dynamic that can exist between the "Child-I" and Central "I" is one in which the Child distrusts the Central "I" and therefore keeps itself distant. There can be several reasons for this distrust on the part of the Child. In some cases, as in the following conversation with Dana, her Child revealed that she distrusted Dana because she feared that Dana would not exert the power to stop the Inner Others from the persecution they had leveled at Dana and her. Dana had just been through a process of confronting her Inner Others, telling them how angry she was about the way they intruded in everything, including therapy. Then she became aware of a pit in her stomach:

Dana: There's an undertow that I'm feeling and there's a pit in my stomach. It's like being pulled from under.
Jack: When did it start?
Dana: When I said that I didn't want to be under their thumb.
Jack: What's the connection? It's giving them up, isn't it?
Dana: Yeah.
Jack: What does it mean to give them up?
Dana: In my head I know that I'll be free.
Jack: But what does it mean emotionally? You literally have a gut reaction when you suggest to yourself to give them up. As we've explored before, that gut reaction relates to a sense of loneliness, doesn't it?
Dana: Yes, that's true.
Jack: Well, where is your Girl right now? Where is she when she hears, "I don't want them. I don't want to be under their thumb"?
Dana: I can't even find her right now. But she was here earlier.
Jack: What do you suppose that means?
Dana: That's when the disowning takes place.
Jack: But I think that is also when she becomes frightened. Do you think that is what is happening also?
Dana: Yes, I think that is what is happening, Jack.
Jack: Then I think she sends out a signal right from here [the solar plexus] which is a communication of the fear. What do you think?
Dana: Yes, I think that is very true.
Jack: Well, I think it would be important to find out what she's afraid of. Maybe it would be helpful if you asked her at this point what it is she is afraid of.
Dana: "What are you afraid of?" [Pause.] It's loneliness, Jack. Because they are always saying, "See, I told you so." I don't trust people. Because of that she's terrified of being alone

because that's my response to people. I end up being alone and so does she.

Jack: Well, why does she get afraid when you suggest giving them up?

Dana: "Why do you get afraid when I talk about giving them up?" She says that then she'll be all alone because there'll be no one left.

Jack: But what about you?

Dana: Me?

Jack: Sure, you can be her friend, can't you? Maybe she's forgotten about that.

Dana: "What about me?" [Pause.] There's a big question mark with that.

Jack: What's the question mark?

Dana: "Well, can you prove it to me?"

Jack: Can you? Do you care for her?

Dana: Do I care for the Child? Yes, I think so.

Jack: What's her reaction to that?

Dana: Umm, I don't know that she believes me.

Jack: Well, ask her if she does.

Dana: Well, she looks at me like . . .

Jack: Like what?

Dana: Like a question mark again.

Jack: It looks like we've discovered something very important here, doesn't it? If your Little Girl doesn't trust you because of your alliance with your Inner Others and she runs from you because of that, it's going to be difficult for the two of you to come together again, isn't it?

Dana: Yes, it is.

Jack: And if that is the case, then you will remain split and at the mercy of your Inner Others, won't you?

Dana: Yes, and I don't like that idea very much.

Jack: Well, it looks like you've got a job here, namely, that you've got to demonstrate to your Child that you value her and that you are willing to own her in spite of what they have to say, and you're going to have to show her that not just occasionally but as an established part of the way you regard her.

Dana: Yes, I think that is true, but that is going to be very hard to do.

Jack: Yes, I agree it's going to be hard, but I think it will pay off in the long run.

Precisely because Dana had so regularly and intensely sided with the Father, Mother, and Aunt, the Child had come to believe it was not possible to have connectedness and alliance with Dana as Central "I." Because the Inner Others aimed their primary barrages at this "bad" part of Dana and because these were designed to rob the Child of its identity and life-force, they were experienced as enemies, threateners of life in the extreme. Because Dana had so identified who she was, the source of her power and value as a person, with these figures, the Child saw her as a threat, which also made it difficult for the Child to trust Dana. If Dana could rearrange her psychological energy so that what she had expended on winning over the parental figures was instead expended on winning over the trust of this inner Child, the sense of inner void, disconnectedness, aimlessness, anxiety could finally be resolved into a general sense of integrity, wholeness, and peace with herself.

Chris had a much deeper distrust of his Child and, as it turns out, his Child of him. The following session reveals the depth of this rift between Chris and his Boy:

Jack: *Who* do you think is angry?
Chris: The Little Boy in me.
Jack: Can you see him?
Chris: I see a Child who's crept into a corner. He's all curled up.
Jack: What's going on with that Child curled up in a corner?
Chris: He's withdrawn and angry. Pulled away. Unreachable.
Jack: Is he that unreachable?
Chris: Well, he is because, uh, inside there's a decision . . . that no one can take away from him.
Jack: Which is what?
Chris: Not to let me or anyone else reach out to him.
Jack: What's the basis for that decision?
Chris: [Pause.] He's not going to do it; he won't.
Jack: Do what?
Chris: He won't let me or anybody reach him. . . .
Jack: Maybe he thinks you're going to take away his right to be over in the corner.
Chris: [Pause.] In effect, I *am* taking away his right to be angry. I don't want to be angry in that corner, so I'm demanding that he not be angry either. I'm saying that my needs are more

important than his. My right to be comfortable is more important than his right to be mad.

Jack: Is there another position you can take?

Chris: I could, uh, let him stay there, let him come to me in his time.

Jack: How would you do that?

Chris: I could say to him, "I understand your anger, and I'm here to comfort you if you want it. I'll wait quietly and if you want to come to me you can." [Pause.] There's something that's not speakable.

Jack: What is it?

Chris: [Pause.] One reason for his anger is his refusal to voice the anger. It's the way he remains in control. He pushes away. "Leave me alone. I'll be angry if I want to and I won't tell you. I don't *have* to tell you."

Jack: Well, he doesn't. That's true. But it must be lonely over there . . .

Chris: [Beginning to sob.] You're right . . . it's lonely over there. [Pause, crying.] That's the magic word. Lonely.

Jack: What happens to the Boy when he hears that word?

Chris: He recognizes the truth. And, uh, his needs change.

Jack: Tell me about that.

Chris: Well, when you said "lonely"—[half laughing, half crying] instead of feeling . . . anger . . . he recognized that . . . that his feelings are deeper than that. When he's angry he feels . . . alone. That's what it's really about.

Jack: So where does that leave him?

Chris: Angry and lonely. [Long silence.]

Jack: What did it mean to him to hear me say "lonely"?

Chris: [Beginning to cry again.] It meant that somebody besides him knew—knew what was really going on—knew what he was feeling. . . . And there was a release inside . . . the anger was gone. It went away. [He claps his hands.] Just like that. [Pause.] And then there were tears. Instead of anger there was . . . there was . . . just in the tears alone there was recognition of . . . of . . .

Jack: Being touched?

Chris: Yeah. Like an arrow piercing the heart!

Jack: So why are you so invested in demanding that the Child not be angry?

Chris: Because I'm afraid that he is going to take over. And if he takes over, the anger runs amuck, then I'm going to be in big trouble.

Jack: In what ways is the Boy going to take over?

Chris: For me to be sitting in a place where I'm angry and I don't know what I'm angry about and that's my state of . . . of feeling, he's in control I would say. [He laughs.]

Jack: So, is there any other way you can attempt to stop the anger besides telling him not to be angry?

Chris: I mean . . . just to recognize . . . to recognize his right to be angry. But the trouble is he doesn't have a right to be angry inside of me, not here, now.

Jack: Who says so?

Chris: I do.

Jack: Why doesn't he have a right to be angry? Why doesn't he have a right to feel what he feels?

Chris: Because that puts him in control of me. When I'm sitting at a table and I'm feeling angry and I recognize there's no clear situation out there for me to be angry at, then. . . .

Jack: No, that's not what's in control of you.

Chris: Oh, the psychic event or attack that has happened inside of me and he *is* angry at that. *That's* where the anger stems from.

Jack: That's right. So therefore, does he have a right to be angry at the attack?

Chris: Yes, he does.

Jack: Yeah, and does he have any other right as a weak and vulnerable Child?

Chris: To comfort.

Jack: Yeah, and if something infinitely more powerful than he is attacking him?

Chris: He has a right to protection.

Jack: That's right. And who's going to give him the protection?

Chris: [Long pause.] He hasn't gotten much. [He laughs.]

Jack: Who's the only person around to give him the protection?

Chris: Me.

Jack: Umhmm.

Chris: So I agree with my Internal Mother.

Jack: That's right.

Chris: She says that he's bad and whatever he wants is bad and everything he eats is bad and that he must be kept under control or otherwise he'll run crazy, hurt himself, or something else.

Jack: What's the result with him when that is all that he hears?

Chris: He goes crazy because he's so hemmed in.

Jack: But what happens when you protect him from that nagging and attacking and you or someone makes a move to understand him? What happened in this session?

Chris: He gives up the anger. He doesn't seem to need it. It doesn't matter anymore. The anger is not important. He ends up choosing because he has a choice instead of being told. He can forget about being angry *and* lonely.

Jack: So what happens? Does her prediction come true, that he will run amuck?

Chris: Nothing happens except that I'm at peace and the war's over.

Jack: So what do you make of that?

Chris: She . . . She's lying!

Jack: So, what do you make of all this?

Chris: There's resolution finally. There can be peace within myself.

Jack: Yep. It all depends on who you want to listen to inside of yourself and who you want to ally yourself with, doesn't it?

Chris: [Laughing] That makes sense. That explains the times in my life when I have been at peace with myself.

The battle lines are clearly drawn in both directions between Chris as Central "I" and the Boy. The Boy had come to distrust Chris because he had unwittingly set himself up as a collaborator with his Internal Mother who, if she had her way, would wipe out the Boy because of the anger contained within him. On the other side, though, Chris had become very much invested in storming and penetrating the protecting castle of the Boy (originally built to save the Boy from the historical-mother) with the intent of destroying it. He hoped the Boy's anger might be wiped out. Because that was Chris's agenda, he failed to understand who was the real and appropriate object of the anger: the violating, depreciating, Internal Mother. On the other hand, because he had identified the Boy as the enemy—the Boy who, ironically, was trying desperately to save their common life from obliteration by the maternal takeover—the Boy more deeply entrenched himself within his psychic castle and became more profoundly unavailable to anyone, *especially* Chris.

So radical was the split between the Boy and Chris that the Boy essentially lost contact with the outside world. Chris's ability to test reality as a total organism was severely curtailed.

Most of the faculties that were available to him to test reality, such as his anger, were not available to him because they were encapsulated and imprisoned in the persona of the Boy. Therefore, much of what the Boy experienced was the constant attack from within by the Internal Mother and Chris himself. Because that was its experience of intimate others, what was happening within the confines of the psyche ended up being projected out onto the external world.

The healing of the rift began when I helped Chris become aware of and acknowledge the Boy as the center of his apparently unresolvable and incomprehensible rage. Once that initial step took place, the open, conscious dialogue began between the two as they started to air the grievances they had toward each other.

There is still another dynamic that affects the continuance of the rupture between the Central and encapsulated "I." Whether the Central "I" distrusts the Child or the Child distrusts the Central "I," the effect is the same: the splitting and disintegration of the total "I," the Self. In addition to the Central "I's" alliance with the Inner Others, there is another and very important factor that keeps these two parts of the Self at odds with each other, distrusting each other. Because the pain is so intense in what appears to be an irreconcilable conflict between the two, and because the feelings that reside in the Child are so intense, when they are available to the Central "I" at any level—such as Chris's awareness of the disconnected anger—they are so overwhelming and painful to it that the Central "I" anesthetizes itself against the pain through more radical splitting off and disowning of it. But the feelings are there to inform the organism that there is some event happening to it. A person dedicated to disconnecting from the warning category of feelings (pain, anger, sadness, etc.) is in a very vulnerable, defenseless, and dangerous situation.

The third relationship between the Central "I" and the Child is one in which the Central "I" hesitates to approach the Child because it fears that the Child will reject it. As a result, the Central "I" experiences itself as irreparably fractured. In the following session with Dana, this clearly emerges as being one of the conflicts around which she had difficulty moving to form an alliance with her Girl. She had been trying to make contact with the Girl but the Inner Others were getting in the way by telling her that this was just a silly exercise which has aroused feelings of embarrassment in her. In response to this she has just yelled back at them.

Jack: How do you feel now that you've realized what was going on?

Dana: There's still a sense of rejection of some sort. It's the kind of thing that I experience in relation to other people a lot.

Jack: Well, let's explore that a little bit.

Dana: Well, supposing I put my arm around her and she would back off. But then I get, "If you don't do it. . . ." It's the old routine, "If you don't do anything, you never get anywhere."

Jack: That sounds like an expectation from your Parents. Has that been an experience of your Little Girl? Has she ever pushed you away when you talked with her or offered to hold her?

Dana: No, that's never happened.

Jack: Well, maybe it's important if you are to see whether your Parents are again seducing you into believing that something is true that is not by asking her to come over. What do you think?

Dana: Well, it's certainly worth a try. They've certainly done that in the past and when I've listened to the lies I've always lost out. [Pause.] "Would you like to come over and have me hold you?"

Jack: What does she say?

Dana: [Smiling softly.] She's come over and sitting in my lap. [She indicates that the Child's head is nestled in her shoulder.] It feels so peaceful . . . whole.

Because of the propaganda from the Inner Others, Dana has come to believe that the automatic response toward her by the other will be rejection. This expectation has ironically included her Child. But as she articulates this subconscious assumption, she is able to see that it comes from the Inner Others and *not* from the Child. She is then able to choose to invite her over and discover that there is an immediate response on her part, that she moves immediately to intimacy with Dana, which evokes a deep sense of peace and wholeness, so unlike the anxiety-ridden relationship with the Inner Others.

The "I" Need vs. the Parental Demand

In an attempt to understand what brought Dana to the standstill that characterized her life and the profound loneliness and isolation of Chris that precipitated both of them to seek therapeutic help, we have separated out the individual personae who comprised the different points of the conflict that resulted in the painful dysfunction of their lives. The individual parts do not make up the whole, however. If we are to understand fully how Dana and Chris found themselves in the psychological predicament they did, we must appreciate how these psychic personae interacted. We end up with a triangle in which the energy flows in all directions, toward and away from each point of the triangle:

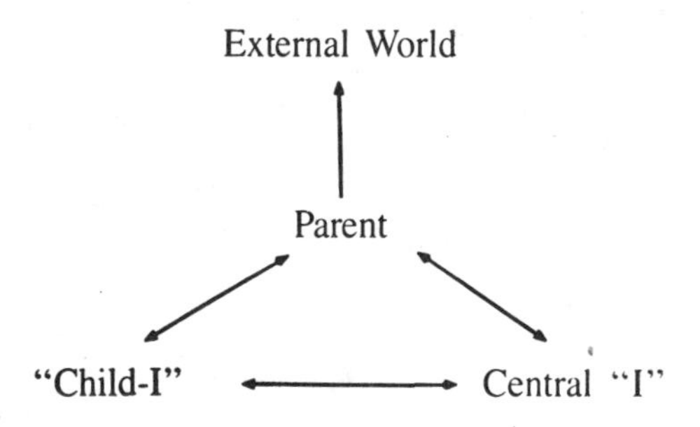

Because the energy of this system is constantly in flux, the Self finds itself where the primary concentration of energy flow is found. If we return to the first conversation with Dana (Chapter 2), the dynamics of the interrelationship between Dana as Central "I," the Child, and the Inner Others are clarified.

On the surface it would seem, as Dana herself put it, "I don't know what I want to do!" Because this is what she believed, that is what happened. She spent much of the day largely consumed by immobility. If we scratch a little below the surface, though, Dana's apparent inability to know what she wanted was not completely accurate. She *did* say, just prior to that, "I wanted to play with my plants—I just wanted to putter with my hands." Therefore, Dana's belief that she couldn't define her life needs, wants, and activities wasn't entirely accurate. What really was happening was that she was ambivalent about what she wanted to do. The ambivalence emerged out of the struggle between the inner personae who were vying for power. It was Dana's ambivalence about who she as Central "I" would ally herself with that brought about the immobilization. She maintained the ambivalence by not deciding which specific task she might or might not perform. By not deciding, she was attempting to maintain an alliance with the Child pulling in one direction and the Inner Others pulling in the other.

At that point in Dana's psychological history, she was forced into the position of maintaining the unconscious balancing act between herself as Central "I," the Inner Others, and her Girl.

The most apparent level of this "balancing act" was the one in which the Child maintained the identity of the "I" in its totality (Central "I" *and* "Child-I") by its rebellious response to the Inner Others. This took several forms. The first level was the outright refusal: "No I won't!—get up—write those letters—water the plants—walk the dog." The second level of the rebellion was in the pleading for mercy through sickness, nausea, and throwing up. The message from the Child to the Inner Other as well as the Central "I" was, "See, I'm *so* sick you couldn't expect me to do what you want me to do. You wouldn't attack someone as weak, sick, and vulnerable as I am, would you?" In the immobility of the illness, the Child had apparently won a victory but it was the victory of the kamikaze pilot who must lose his life to sink the enemy's ship. The Child maintained the identity of the "I" but at the expense of life-giving activity. Life had become for Dana a series of battles of which this was a mere singular example in which the outcome was a miserable grey and bland form of existence dominated by frustrating immobility, a kind of living death.

Another session with Dana and a series of events surrounding that session showed how intense this battle was. Over a period of months, Dana had been complaining of an increasing sense of pressure and pain around her trachea (windpipe) and esophagus in which she had difficulty both swallowing and breathing. A short time before this session, she was rushed to the emergency facility of a hospital by her husband because it was so severe. She was released after a few hours when there did not seem to be anything organically wrong (such as a heart attack, although that was suspected). But a few weeks after this, she had another attack which required about a week of hospitalization in which it was determined that the esophagus had collapsed because of anxiety and tension. When she started the session, she had complained of a great deal of pressure in the throat region in which she found it difficult to both swallow and breathe. In our conversation some of the conflicts emerged that are behind a great deal of this pressure. Here she was talking about having had a party and what was happening to her during the party:

Dana: I was a hostess. I should go around and greet everybody. They all knew me.
Jack: What do you mean, you "should" go around?
Dana: Well, that was my . . . like they all know me.
Jack: That doesn't really explain the "should."
Dana: Well, it was my party and that's what I always do. Oh, I see, the "should." Yeah. [Pause.] Well, many of the people I met from the beginning of the year, many friends—and uh—I like to mix in, I really do. It was a chore on Friday [the day of the party]. Today was the same. "Now, you can't hang back." It really hurt me to talk and then I was tired. I'm always tired. I didn't do that much that would tire me out. . . . But I think the whole thing of it was, you know, the worry of it, "I'm not going to make this." And I want to.
Jack: What is the worry? Where does that come from?
Dana: You should and you better. Uh—You're supposed to.
Jack: You're supposed to be taking care of these people?
Dana: Take care of people, greet them and—I was all worn out by five o'clock. And then this thing that was so new, like that time I went into the hospital. I had that again yesterday. I didn't want to be home because they [the guests] would be asking for me and what they would say is, "She's sick again." [Said with a disgusted tone of voice.]

The Triangle—Slavery vs. the Fight for Life

Of course the guests would not have criticized her for being ill and since no one ever made any kind of remark to that effect, the idea had to come from somewhere else—inside Dana's head. The somewhere was her Internal Aunt, who, as we have seen before, criticized her any time she felt ill. In addition to her Aunt, Dana's Internal Mother was also present in the statement, "You should go around (and be responsible for everyone's having a good time)." Thus the anger that she was aware of was not really toward herself for not feeling well but toward the two internal persons who were harping at her from inside. As that anger came too close to the surface, the lid was put on at the point that the anger might pop out, at the Adam's apple, the voice box—thus the pain in the windpipe. Realizing the Little Girl was probably someplace in this internal interaction, I asked Dana:

Jack: Where is your Little Girl in this issue of the party? Where do you see her in this room [my office]?

Dana: She's over in the corner, sitting on the floor with her head down. She seems to be very sad.

Jack: Ask her what she's doing in the corner.

Dana: "Little Girl, what are you doing in the corner?" [Pause.] She says she can never have a good time because they're always nagging and because I won't do anything about it.

Jack: Well, what do you make of that?

Dana: She's right, they are constantly nagging and I *don't* do anything about it. I get lost and overwhelmed.

Jack: Maybe it would be helpful if you could get her to come over to you so you could talk it over. Do you want to do that?

Dana: Yes. "Little Girl, do you want to come over and have me hold you while we talk?" [Pause.]

Jack: What's her response?

Dana: She's hesitant but coming.

Jack: Has she come yet?

Dana: Yes.

Jack: Why don't you ask her what she is hesitant about?

Dana: "Why were you hesitant?" [Pause.] She says she doesn't really know if I want her.

Jack: Do you?

Dana: Yes!

Jack: Maybe it would help if you told her that and why you want her.

Dana: "I really want you here because without you I feel very lost and empty, and when you are here with me I feel happy."

Jack: How does she respond to that?

Dana: She's very happy about that and not so sad anymore.

Jack: How does she respond to that?

Dana: She's very happy about that and not so sad anymore.

Jack: Does that say anything to you?

Dana: Yes, that I ignore that part of me and she's very sad, but if I acknowledge her and invite her over, the sadness disappears.

Jack: Right! Now that she's here, you can ask her where she was the night of the party?

Dana: "Where were you the night of the party?" [Pause.] She says she was trying to have a good time but all these demands were being made on her to take care of everybody and she couldn't have a good time.

Jack: Ask her how she felt about that.

Dana: "How did you feel about that?" [Pause.] She says she was angry.

Jack: Ask her about the pain in the throat.

Dana: "What about the pain in the throat? What was going on?" [Pause.] She says she was very angry about not being able to have a good time and the pain in the throat was my not allowing her to be angry.

Jack: I see. What does this say to you?

Dana: It says that I don't allow my anger to happen and because I don't listen to it, it gets stuck in my throat. This is unbelievable!

Jack: Well, I think it would be to your benefit to start believing it.

Dana: Yeah, I guess so.

Although she was aware of being angry, Dana had misidentified the source of criticism as her guests. Further, she had also misidentified herself as the object of the anger since they said (and she believed them) it was she who was "at fault" because she was not feeling well. Her not feeling well became the focal point of her anger, a hook onto which it could be hung, because it matched the Aunt's attack. This was also convenient because the guests could have been the object of the anger, since, in her mind, they were criticizing her "for being sick." But by identifying the object of the anger as the sickness (therefore herself), the encapsulated anger contained within the Little Girl stayed within and therefore out of sight. The Central "I" was convinced that the anger must be disowned at all costs, even to the point of inflicting bodily harm!

As the inner attack mounted, Dana's Child more frantically and strenuously fought for life. The more she fought, the more she was admonished by her Internal Mother and Aunt and pushed down by Dana. Thereby the pressure for survival mounted. The Little Girl fell back on the only tactic she had—open rebellion through pounding away at the door, the voice box in the throat, until somebody acknowledged her. Dana was repeatedly forced to do this every time she collapsed or was carted off to the hospital with these severe symptoms. Something had to give. If Dana had been able to recognize the psychological seesaw she was involved in, her body could not have continued to suffer the kind of punishment it was getting because of that inner conflict.

Dana had also lost track of life. In this specific incident, because of the Little Girl's battle for survival before the parental onslaught, the occasion of the party had become a battlefield. Instead of having fun and enjoying being with her friends, Dana saw her friends as enemies who were out to destroy her under the weight of criticism and responsibility. Because of all this, Dana could not participate in the life of the party but through her Child was fighting for survival of identity or, to put it another way, trying to prevent the loss of identity or avoiding death.

When she turned to examine what was happening inside, this all changed. The party and her not feeling well had been turned into issues by the Aunt and Mother. Dana now had the *real* problem defined and could begin moving toward resolution. With the discovery of the activity of the Internal Parents, the activity of the Little Girl was implicated. And so she was. Once that participant was brought into the conscious conversation, Dana was on the home stretch. As the Little Girl and Dana were united once again and the party and the friends were divested of appearing to comprise the enemy camp, Dana as a unified Self was now in a position to stop struggling for life, and, instead, live life.

The parts do not make the whole. The whole is the engagement of parts and the alliances in that engagement, as well as the major focus of power in that triangle. If the subject understands that it can achieve control over this dynamic, inner process by wresting the power from the inner images and joining forces with the inner Child, life can be peaceful, wholesome and fun—most of the time—and not a struggle of avoiding death.

Part V

HEALING THE FRACTURE

9

THE HEALING FROM WITHIN

The Decision Maker

The cornerstone to the process of healing the Self resides within the Central "I." If the developing child were able to exist without any psychological conflict during the developmental time, the Central "I" and "Child-I" would not come to be separate entities. Rather, these two psychological entities, which operate as disconnected and warring parties, would instead function as a unified whole.

When the Self is split into parts, as it is in most of us, what is contained in the "Child-I" is not available to the Central "I" in its functioning and vice versa. For instance, Chris radically disowned his anger and encapsulated it within his disowned Little Boy. But anger was thus lost to Chris as a part of his psychological apparatus for functioning in the world. Because the anger was unavailable to him in his day-to-day functioning, Chris as Central "I" experienced himself as defenseless against violations and threats from without, and as supremely vulnerable in relationship to others. To cope with that vulnerability, he retreated from the world.

If, however, the Self is not broken down into these separate, non-communicative parts, we have a very different picture:

when there is or appears to be an attack against the person from the outside, the Self is able to listen to the aroused anger, to mobilize into action and to defend itself against the violation or intrusion from the outside.

The objective, then, in the healing process is to bring into unity and harmony what existed in disunity and disharmony. To accomplish this, the divisive presence and force of the Inner Other must be recognized as such and cast out.

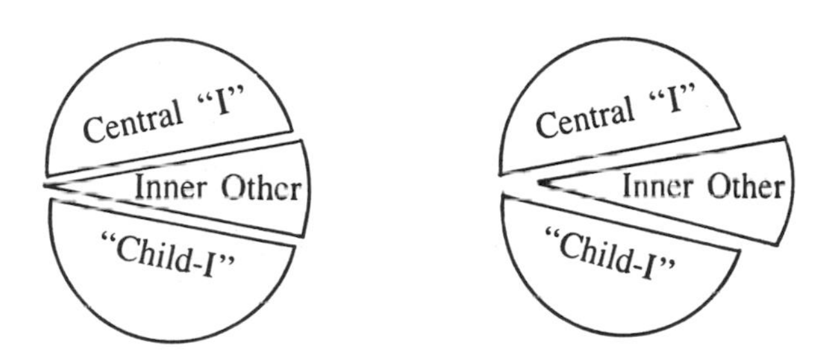

Once that is achieved, although the wall between the Central "I" and the "Child-I" is gone, they remain separate and disintegrated. This, in turn, must be addressed. That gulf must be healed as well. When the healing is complete, the Central "I" and "Child-I" cease to exist as separate, disunited entities. Rather, they merge or fuse into one, harmonious, unified being of the Self.

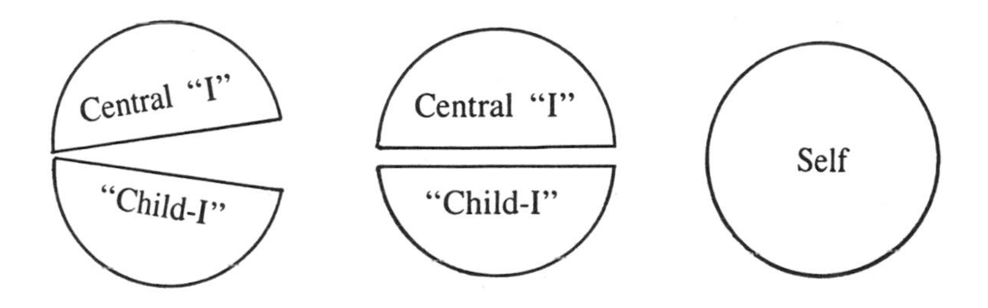

The power to achieve this reunification of the Self resides within the Central "I." If, therefore, the process of healing is to be fully understood and achieved, the nature, function, and powers of the Central "I" must be understood as well. To understand these, it is necessary to understand the Self in its individual state, from which the Central "I" is derived.

At the very center of the nature and power of the Self is its ability to be aware of itself as being: I-am-aware-that-I-am. To bring the Self into that self-aware state and to maintain and protect it, there are clustered within and around the Self a broad variety of functions.

The first of these are feeling states. The feeling states serve two functions. First, they inform the unified Self whether it is in danger or not. The feelings break down into two categories: warning feelings and well-being feelings. Warning feelings, such as anger, fear, or anxiety, warn the Self that there is some danger that threatens its existence or well-being, and motivate the Self to deal with the danger. Well-being feelings, such as peace, joy, or happiness, on the other hand, inform the Self that all is well.

The second role the feelings play is to stimulate the Self to become self-aware of its I AM-ness.

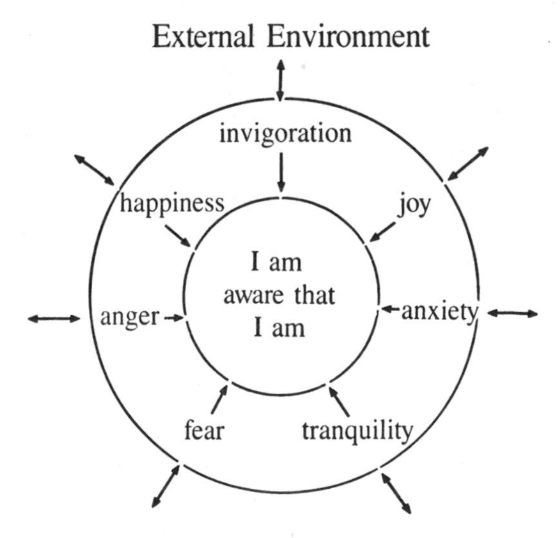

In addition to the feeling states, there are cognitive states. The first among these is the faculty of observation. The observational capability of the Self breaks down into two categories: (1) the ability to observe outside events, for example, I observe that you are reading; and (2) the ability to observe the Self. The ability to observe the Self breaks down into two categories of observations: (1) the ability to observe what the Self is doing within the external environment, for instance, I observe that I am writing; and (2) the ability to observe what is happening within the internal environment, for instance, I observe that I am feeling happy and content.

The second faculty of the Self is the ability to integrate what it is aware of in its observations: I am aware that I am happy and content *because* I am writing.

After the integration, the Self is able to make judgments about itself. Because I am happy and content with writing, I judge that I like to write. Based on that judgment, I enter into the final stage of the process by acting on my judgment: I, in fact, continue to write.

Unfortunately, for many of us, because the Self was so radically split into disparate, warring parties by the introduction of the Inner Other during childhood, this apparently simple, straightforward process has been turned into a very complex, disruptive one.

The Intrusion Now

As long as the Central "I" or "Child-I" believes that the source of identity and power resides in the Inner Other, the subject will remain split asunder, without a sense of integrity, power, or control over its own life and destiny. If, on the other hand, the subject acknowledges the Internal Parent as an entity separate and distinct from itself, who presents a mostly untrue and distorted picture of itself and the outside world, the subject then is in a position to challenge the authority and power of this internal figure.

Most definitely Dana and Chris were victims of their Inner Others. They believed that these internal figures were absolute in their knowledge, authority, and power over them. Because they never had a chance to challenge the absoluteness of their original parenting figures from whom the final, internal images had been shaped, these internal personae were never challenged either. The original assumptions about the absolute power and irreplaceability of these figures remained intact as well. The result was that in spite of the ever-increasing pain they found themselves living in, it never occurred to them to question or change this order of things.

With therapy, however, they were introduced to the reality of the Inner Others as psychological entities, separate and distinct from the Self, to the hitherto unchallenged assumptions about the absolute power and irreplaceability of these internal figures, and to the possibility of other ways of assessing the Self and the world around it. This served both to weaken the Inner Others in their position of absolute authority over Chris and Dana and to help them build up their own sense of power and authority over themselves. This required, however, an examination on the part of these two people of what happened to them when the internal personae were present and active within them.

To begin with, Dana and Chris discovered that the presence and activity of their Inner Others generated whole categories of feelings that were very unpleasant. Many of these feelings seemed to erupt out of nowhere, confusing and baffling Dana and Chris about their origin and, ultimately, their resolvability. Finally, though, Dana was able to connect her monumental anxiety, guilt, inner sense of worthlessness, immobility, and bodily manifestations in the form of headaches, severe intestinal problems, and especially the very painful and frightening collapse of her esophagus to their activity. Chris, too, was finally able to find and attach to the activity of his Internal Mother a cause as well as an agent of his intense sense of inner loneliness, isolation, and monumental rage.

Once they were able to identify these inner personae as the origin and cause of these hitherto unattachable feeling states and the impact they had on their ability to function, they were able to extract the wedge that had splintered them apart. With their inner obstacles out of the way, they were now in a position to acknowledge, address, and carry on a new conversation with their other sides. It was the loss of these parts of themselves—parts that had been shoved aside by the images of the all-powerful and all-knowing Other—that had created the inner sense of emptiness, valuelessness, loneliness, and isolation that both Dana and Chris had experienced within themselves. Once they had regained access to these lost, original parts, the feelings that flowed out of that psychological vacuum could be healed.

Because they had assumed the validity of the original order of things (I am the weaker one who is always at the mercy of the all-important and powerful Other), and because they had "forgotten" about the original splitting up of the Self and the taking inside of a Trojan horse filled with enemies, their relationships with their Inner Others became more valid, real, and intense than their relationships with other people.

Chris's deep sense of loneliness emerged because all he could hear from inside were his mother's charges of "Garbage!" Dana believed that she must know what was going on inside the Other without asking because her Inner Other voices demanded this of her, otherwise she would not be loved and would thereby be destroyed. Both lived in a foggy world of mirages created by these internal voices. Although it appeared to them that they were engaging someone in their external environment, they frequently *really* were engaging their Internal Parents.

Because these inner figures made the world of outside persons appear to be hostile, thereby making them into enemies who would overwhelm and obliterate them whenever they could, Dana and Chris experienced enormous anxiety whenever they anticipated or attempted to engage any outside person. This, of course, only served to advance and reaffirm the protective walls against the outside, apparently "hostile" world. This, in turn, left them even more alone with the real enemy, the Inner Others.

The discovery of these Inner Other voices as concrete, real, and active personae that had an existence separate and distinct from themselves as subjects gave them a very powerful tool toward resolving the internal conflicts that disrupted their everyday lives. The activity of the Inner Others and the splitting of the Self is an event very much rooted in the present. True, the roots to its existence and activity are buried in the "ancient" developmental history of the individual. The activity of the Inner Other, however, is not a past event but one that occurs in the here and now, disrupting it, often severely, in the present time.

Recognizing the present reality of the Inner Other and its activity adds a new dimension to the psychotherapeutic process. This insight into the unconscious processes treats these processes as happening now and not as happening in the distant, clouded past of the individual. Undoubtedly there is value in remembering the conditions of that clouded past. Certainly it does help the individual to recognize events that were overwhelming and unresolvable within the conditions of childhood—events which were repressed, but now can be seen in the new light of adulthood. There are, however, a couple of problems to a therapeutic approach that concentrates exclusively on past events.

First, no one—not the subject, the parent, the therapist, or even God—can change the events of the past. Second, remembering the historical event does not address the now-present dialogue that keeps the old belief systems alive, since the historical events and conditions live on in the internalized images. Thus, once the subject has remembered and addressed the historical event, an event which no one can change, the subject is still left with the intense, ongoing, real, but unrecognized, present, inner personae and events. There cannot be any resolution to what is happening in the present: the ghosts do not disappear simply because we visit the site of the original crime through reminiscences. The violations against the subject can only stop when each subsequent crime is recognized and addressed as it is committed by the present, internal enemy. Of course, exploring the historical roots wherein these Inner Others were formed and began the original dialogue can be very helpful in the understanding and resolutions of the present-day, internal dialogue. History taking alone, however, does not go very far in rearranging the present-day, internal dialogue so that it does not rule, overpower, and diminish the Self.

Certainly it is helpful to acknowledge the reality of the internal dialogue no matter what label is attached to it, because with the acknowledgment comes the possibility of challenging the assumptions of the dialogue. However, regarding the Inner Other only as another state of the "I" means that the anger and other feelings that are generated from the interaction between the different "I" states (Central "I" and "Child-I") and the

Inner Other end up being aimed at the Self. If the Inner Other, on the other hand, is recognized and addressed as the internal object it is (by virtue of the fact that it addresses the subject "I" as a "you"), the anger or other feelings can be aimed at something other than itself. This recognition of the Inner Other as object and not as a part of the subject frees the "I" to rely on its own powers, faculties, and experiences and allows it to give up its belief that it needs this other authority to survive.

Three Sets of Parents

When we speak of parents, it is important that we distinguish between three possible meanings of the term. There are our parents of the past (historical-parents), our parents in the present (now-parents), and our Inner Others (Internal Parents). For all of us the model(s) for the Inner Other were the Important Others of mother, father, aunt, uncle, brother, sister, Mrs. Smith from next door, or perhaps a teacher or religious figure. Therefore, the proper name of our Inner Other takes on the name of those from whom we modeled that internal image. Because that was our historical, developmental history, the distinctions between the historical parental model, the internal parental Other, and the now-parent become blurred.

As was said earlier, the events of history are unalterable and unchangeable. This includes the persons of history. None of us can reverse an act that has been done in the past. The best we can do is to change the decision that was made then, to something else now. That does not change the past event. What it does do is to stop the "ripples" out of the past and create new "ripples" that in turn move to a future time. So too it is with the persons of the past. Their activity, as well as the intentionality behind their acts in history, is unalterable now by anyone, including themselves. They can reaffirm what they did or who they were, or they can apologize. But, regardless of what they do now, they can never alter who they were then. That includes our Important Other figures of the past.

On the other side of that is who and what we are or choose to be today. I can act today on the same beliefs and values on which I acted ten, fifteen, twenty-five years ago. If that is what I choose to do, consciously or unconsciously, that is what and who I am *today.* If, on the other hand, I decide to alter my beliefs and values and act on that alteration, then that is who and what I become *today.* So too it is with our Important Other figures of our history. They can either hold onto what they believed and valued twenty, forty, sixty years ago, and that is who they are—*today.* On the other hand, they can examine and change attitudes and values of yesteryear, throw some out, keep some, and formulate new ones. When they do that, that is who they are—*today.*

More often than not, the inability on the part of adult offspring to recognize the futility of pursuing an unavailable parent is blocked by the Inner Other who says: "How can you abandon your father/mother that way? You should be ashamed of yourself after all he/she has done for you." When that happens, the external reality of the now-parent gets confused and blurred with the reality of the Inner Other who speaks as the original parental figure spoke.

This was Chris's problem at the outset of therapy. His now-mother had continued to treat him in a very despicable way with a continuing barrage of insults or stony silence when he wouldn't give her everything she wanted from him. His Internal Mother blamed him for the attacks and excused the now-mother. It was only when we separated who was saying what that Chris was able to realize how hopeless it was for him to expect anything, especially respect, from his now-mother. The more he pursued that end, the less he would have available for more appropriate relationships. On the other side of that, he came to realize how much his Internal Mother blocked out the reality and significance of his now-mother's behavior and attitudes toward him.

On the other hand, the Internal Parent can blur the now-parent who is making other choices than it had made in the past. Because the historical parent was the original model for the Internal Parent and because there is a continuity between historical-parent and now-parent, the real alterations in attitudes and behavior toward the adult offspring can often be confused.

Earlier, we saw how Dana's mother had continued to treat her like a disobedient child when Dana tried to work out a compromise with her about going to church. At that point in her therapeutic process she was not able to confront her mother. Dana ended up responding the way she would have as a child, with a great deal of guilt, repressed thoughts and feelings about what happened, and capitulation to her mother. Since that time, however, she had been confronting her now-mother about that kind of behavior and the attitudes behind it, and her mother had seen that she was acting inappropriately and had worked to change it. Nevertheless, it had taken Dana some time to catch up with what was really going on. The following is a session in which Dana had slipped into the confusion between her Internal Mother and her now-mother. (Dana is talking about how she was hoping that her mother wouldn't call her because she wanted to watch a particular TV program.)

Jack: Why did you hope that she wouldn't call as the show was beginning?

Dana: I didn't want to miss the show. See, then I would have felt. . . . See, that was it . . . I could have. . . .

Jack: You would have felt . . . ?

Dana: [Long pause.] I guess . . . uh . . . hmm . . . the first thought that comes into my mind is just being polite enough to stay on the phone but that's really not thinking that much of myself to want to really see the value I had in watching that.

Jack: So who says it's not polite to say to your mother, "Hey, Mom, X program is just starting. It's important to me. How about if I call you when it's over?"

Dana: My Internal Mother tells me I wouldn't do that.

Jack: OK, what do you want to say back?

Dana: "What's important to me *counts!* Not what you want." If *I* want to call her back later, I can.

Jack: That's right. And what do you think your flesh-and-blood mother would say anyway if you said that to her?

Dana: She'd probably say, "OK."

Jack: Yeah.

Dana: She probably would.

Jack: Exactly. So what do you want to say to your Internal Mother?

Dana: "Just quit projecting yourself on my mother! You are *not* my mother!"

Jack: And what happens because of that?

Dana: You make her diminish.

Jack: That's right. She's not there for you.

Dana: I don't see her there as a person then.

Dana was now beginning to realize that it was not her now-mother who was so powerful and important but the Internal Mother. Because she had misidentified who her enemy really was, it was impossible to bring about a resolution of her problem and the tension it brought with it. As time went on after this session and she became aware of how often and how much the Internal Parent(s) interfered with the relationship between herself and her now-mother, she was able to address the intrusion of her Internal Mother. She was then able to tell her now-mother what she needed and wanted. As she did this, she discovered that if she was clear, her now-mother could respect her needs most of the time. This came to change their relationship in a radical way. Dana found that her mother was not as overbearing as she had originally believed her to be. Rather, she could often be very sympathetic and responsive to Dana.

Healing the Void—Claiming the Child

Once the person has realized the significance of the internal interruptions on the part of the Inner Other voice(s) and has begun to challenge and stop them, the person must come to terms with the further reality that a psychological void still remains to be refilled before the underlying split in its psychic life is healed. The psychological space the developing child fashioned to accommodate the newly created Internal Parent was formerly occupied by aspects of the "I" that the child perceived as a threat and danger to it because it was punished in some way by the parent when they were in evidence, at least from the point of view of the child. These "dangerous" parts of the "I" then became encapsulated, cut off, disowned, and repressed.

As long as these aspects of the Self remain cut off, dispossessed and unavailable to the Central "I," it is cut off from major aspects of its life-force. Therefore, if the subject attempts only to depose the Inner Other from its psychic throne without, in turn, refilling the psychic vacuum that is created in that maneuver by restoring the "Child-I" to its rightful and original place, the Self remains weakened because the original split from its own life-force remains intact. The Inner Other will quickly step back into the empty psychological space and assume control over the subject again.

We have had glimpses of the process by which the Child is recognized and reclaimed. The impact this has had on Dana in a session that took place early in her therapeutic journey demonstrates well the dynamics of the interplay between Dana as Central "I," her Little Girl, and the Inner Others. The session reveals with considerable intensity the roadblocks to reunification the Inner Others threw up to prevent Dana from reclaiming the Child and what she had to do to overcome them. By this time in her struggle, she had come to realize her Child was the key to her survival and persevered in doing what she had to do to reclaim herself.

Dana: This morning it was on me again and all the anxiety and I said, "I'm going to work." "No, I'm not going to work!" [Her tone deepens and sounds obstinate.] "Yes, I'm going!" "No, I'm not going!" I went through this routine. "You shouldn't go; you don't feel well."

Jack: "I'm going." "I'm not going." What's being manifested there? What is the pull? Who are the psychic partners there? "I'm going." "I'm not going"? What's the feeling tone to the "I'm not going"?

Dana: That's the Belligerent Child.

Jack: Were you aware of that before?

Dana: No.

Jack: Okay. This is what I'm trying to get you in touch with.

Dana: [With surprise] It wasn't the Parents?

Jack: Right. It was not them.

Dana: That came in later.

Jack: Exactly. Now, let's explore this. When you get yourself into the "I don't want to," what is the feeling tone?

Dana: "Well, now, let's talk this over." Something like that.

Jack: So let's talk it over with her right now.

Dana: "Why don't you want to go to work?" "Because I don't feel good. I'll never get through the day." It's all excuses. [Here the Parent intruded with a put-down and an attack.]

Jack: Who is intruding?

Dana: My Inner Parents.

Jack: OK, can you get back on the track? Can you push it aside and get back in your dialogue with the Little Girl?

Dana: "Now you get out of here! I'm talking to her!"

Jack: Now where were we?

Dana: "Are you sure that you don't feel good? Why don't you feel good?"

Jack: OK, what does she say?

Dana: She says, "Yeah, I don't feel good." Yeah, that's her.

Jack: Now, you know about little children as well as I do. When a little child is feeling or sometimes says, "I am ill," what are they really looking for?

Dana: Affection.

Jack: Can you say, "Come here, I'll soothe you"?

Dana: I don't do so well with that. I'm not very kind, I suppose. [With a command in her voice] "Come over here and we'll talk about it."

Jack: Do you think it might be a good idea to hold her?

Dana: Yeah. I'm not too good at this.

Jack: In what way? How do you feel when you get to this point?

Dana: I feel strange.

Jack: What do you mean, strange?

Dana: A little disconnected.

Jack: Explain that a little bit more.

Dana: Like I want to disconnect from the Other . . . so that's . . .

Jack: Disconnect . . .

Dana: From the parents.

Jack: They're still on the scene then.

Dana: Well, I mean ordinarily, I want to disconnect from them.

Jack: What happens inside as you contemplate bringing the Little Child onto your lap? What is it? It's uneasiness, right?

Dana: Yeah.

Jack: Can you explain that a little more?

Dana: I seem to be able to go just so far.

Jack: Where?

Dana: Here. [To standing in front of her.]

Jack: Then what happens?

Dana: A break.

Jack: What is the break?

Dana: Do I really mean it? [Here it emerged that the Child within really questioned Dana's sincerity.]

Jack: Do *you* really mean it?

Dana: Do I really want to comfort her or . . . ?
Jack: Uh-huh.
Dana: I can't identify with the Little Child. I know what I want to do with them. Get rid of them. This one hasn't been taken care of too well.
Jack: But she's very real, though, isn't she?
Dana: Not as real as they are, though. I forget to look on that area. There *is* a Child. I can see the Child. I *hear* the Child, constantly when I'm down.
Jack: Right. See, you've got to get in touch with her if you want to feel whole again. The presence of your parents caused you to try to get rid of her in your childhood, so you pushed her into the recesses of your unconscious and you've split her off from you. And now you were fighting against her. Mmm?
Dana: I was fighting against her. Yeah.

When Dana originally came into therapy she was becoming aware that she lived a life that was constantly tainted with an undertone of anxiety that had recently begun to build up. The anxiety and other undefinable feelings were reaching the point of getting out of control and were beginning to overwhelm her and render her more and more immobile. By the time this session happened, she was much more aware of the *inner* processes that caused this state of affairs. She was now more able to identify what the feelings were that hitherto had merely churned around inside of her without name and chance of resolution. She had become more able to recognize there were Inner Other thoughts in her mind, too, which had an intimate connection with the dissociated feelings she was feeling.

At this point in her therapeutic journey, though, she still had a very pronounced tendency when by herself to respond to the anxiety states as though they stood alone. My task became one of assisting her to consciously make the connections that were already there and to integrate them. By using the tape and pointing out to her the significance of what she was saying, I was helping her to see what was happening, as a subject who could stand back and observe the inner processes, to objectify herself to herself.

Until now, Dana had depended on the Inner Other personae to objectify her, to observe and make judgments about and to her. Because she had never learned to do this for herself and thereby abdicated herself to this Inner Other authority, she was subject to any observation and judgment it made about her. She was at its mercy and lived a life in which she was merely a satellite. By slowing her down and having her observe, evaluate and judge her own internal events, I was helping her to learn that she could do this on her own. She did not have to depend on the authority of these distorting, deceiving Inner Others.

This was not the last time the Inner Others tried to block Dana from discovering and moving toward reclaiming this little-known part of herself. As each of their blocks and intrusions came, it was important to acknowledge the reality of the activity. Then she had to push them aside, either by angrily pushing them out of the way or by *consciously* turning her back on them and redoubling her efforts at involvement with the Little Girl. What she learned in all of this was that she must fight for this Little Girl and that it was *worth it* to fight for her!

Coming to that realization was a struggle, though. As the internal process unwound in the progression of the session, another important element revealed itself. In the discovery that she felt more at home with the feelings that were generated with the Inner Other figures (that is, guilt, worthlessness, helplessness, and unarticulated and disconnected rage), her tendency to return to them and an inability to let go of them began to make great sense. Her inner void was the product of the absence of a significant part of her own Self, her own life flow, the Child. As long as this part of herself remained cut off and unavailable to her, she had to fill that void with something. Otherwise she would die, or so she thought. This something that filled the void turned out to be the Inner Other.

The turning point came for Dana when she recognized that she had a choice of whom she was going to use to fill up the void, and when she understood what would happen to her depending on which of them she chose—the Inner Other or the Child.

Letting Go

Even as Dana and Chris were fighting to free themselves of their Inner Others by addressing the attack and attacker, there were many subtle ways in which they were trapped and seduced into maintaining the relationship. We worked to overcome four of these binds.

(1) Pleading and begging:

Dana: [Shouting.] "Why don't you stop it?! I've got a constant pain in my stomach. I'm scared stiff with it!"

Jack: Why are you *asking* them to leave? Why don't you *tell* him to get out?

Dana: Yeah, why am I asking him? "You bastard! I hate you! Get out! You make me a child! *Go a-way!"*

Jack: Can you feel the anger toward them?

Dana: No, I can't. Just the pain in my stomach from . . . having so much hatred.

Jack: The pain in your stomach is hatred against yourself and not towards them.

Dana: Yes, that's right. And fear and all the other things.

Jack: You have nothing to fear.

Dana: *"Why-don't-you-stop?"* I keep trying. When am I going to come to an end of this?

Jack: Do you hear how you are begging them to leave you alone? There's a big difference between saying, "Will you please leave me alone?" and, "Get the hell away from me!" Do you hear the difference?

Dana: Yes, I do. I've been begging them to leave and I don't have to beg.

Jack: Well, do you want to attack them rather than be attacked?

Dana: Yes! [At this point Dana gets up out of her chair and stands before the five-foot dummy, nose to nose.] "Dammit to hell! I'm sick and tired of what you do to me!" [She hits the dummy and it falls. She then starts kicking it.] "Get out of here! I hate what you do to me when you are around!"

Jack: How do you feel now?

Dana: I feel a lot better.

When Dana responded to her Internal Parents by pleading with them, she was unconsciously accepting their fundamental assumption that they were more powerful than she; that their presence was more important then anything else; and that she could not acknowledge what they were doing to her in the attack. Once she was able to see what she was doing and refused to go along with the parental assumptions, she was able to attack back.

(2) Apologizing:

Dana: They're on my back again today. I hear them saying, "You're not making it in this therapy." "Well, I'm doing the best I can." Then I feel so guilty. I can't do anything right. It's so exhausting.

Jack: Do you hear the apologizing? Instead of apologizing, what can you say?

Dana: "There is nothing for me to apologize for! You're the ones who make it difficult! All you do is nag me, put me down. Get the hell away from me, you bastards! I'm sick and tired of your guilt and put-downs! Go to hell! This is the place I can get my anger out and you try to take it away from me. You hurt me. You invade my stomach, my head, my legs! I'm not blaming it on anything else but you!"

(3) Convincing:

Dana: "You say I did the job today wrong. Well, I didn't! It turned out OK. Everybody thought that it worked out well. But you keep nagging me about how I did it! You won't leave me alone!"

Jack: Did you hear how you were arguing with it, trying to convince it that you did the job OK? It seems as though you are using the other people's opinion to help in that convincing.

Dana: Yes, I do hear that.

Jack: Is there another way you can respond to its criticism of the way you did the job?

Dana: "I want you to mind your own business. You have no right telling me what to do and how to do it. All you do when you start that garbage is to confuse me and turn everything upside down. So go to hell!"

Jack: So how do you feel now, having said that?

Dana: It feels resolved.

The basic assumption here is that nothing is good enough. Since it's not good enough, she's not good enough. Once that assumption is challenged and disowned, her worth is not at stake and she is freed from the guilt of her frustration.

Chris once expressed his frustrated desire to be brought back into his Internal Mother's favor in the image of being locked out of a spaceship. As he stood there preoccupied with his frustration, he was so engrossed in gaining admittance that the rest of the world seemed to cease to exist, for it appeared to him as a few distant stars immersed in a sea of blackness.

(4) Anger and frustration:

Jack: What would happen if you simply turned around and walked away from her?

Chris: [There was a minute or so of silence, then a smile began to crawl across his face.] You know, I turned away. I started walking away from her. Then I turned my back, the blackness dissolved and everything came alive. There are colors, landscape, trees, birds! It's not all black and empty, but it's alive and full of color!

Jack: Does that say anything to you?

Chris: Yes. It says to me that if I'm caught up in my frustration and anger with her about her non-acceptance of me, then I will be so preoccupied with that that everything else ceases to exist. But if I simply give up fighting for her acceptance and approval and walk away from her, all the energy that I put into that endless and hopeless battle is put into enjoying the real world.

10

HEALING THROUGH OTHERS

Something Better Than Nothing

As Dana progressed through therapy, she was faced with the choice of continuing her relationship with her Internal Parents or of giving them up. On the one hand, to continue to maintain the alliance with the internal parental figures was tantamount to committing suicide, as she was literally strangling herself with unexpressed but appropriate anger. On the other hand, to give them up appeared to her to be the giving up of everything she knew about herself and her world, even life itself. My task was to challenge that perception and to show her that when she reclaimed the real source of her life, her Child, her experience of life would change from one of darkness to one of light.

In one session, Dana had been confronting her Internal Mother both verbally and physically. There was a pause, and then the following exchange:

Dana: I feel like . . . Oh, I feel like I'm sitting here all alone.

Jack: That's her ultimate weapon. That's what prevents you from challenging her statements—the threat of being alone.

Dana: I don't want to walk after her. I'd rather stand alone. I'd rather be lonely for the rest of my life!

Jack: Is that the only option? [Pause.] The fact is, you are not alone. I am here.

Dana: Why can't I absorb that fact?

Jack: There is a part of you that is very much bound to her. You hear her saying, "If you dare to confront me, I will abandon you." Her voice is loud, and you can't turn away from it. When you try, you become fear-stricken, and the Fearful Child emerges. But there is also the Rebellious Child. Between the two of them a conflict emerges when you enter a group situation.

Dana: That's right. That's right.

So intense had Dana's interaction with her Internal Mother been, that to push her out of the way of her relationship with the external world meant that she was leaving a relationship that—though painful, debilitating, and unproductive—was at least there. Dana perceived that she either had to suffer the presence of her Inner Others or she had to be alone. Therefore, she experienced an enormous resistance to autonomy and independence.

Chris, in his image of being locked out of the spaceship, presented a similar conflict. He was so preoccupied with being taken back into his Internal Mother's world that it seemed to be the only goal and activity in life. To express his anger toward her for the way she had violated him would only prolong the banishment. Because of this, the rest of the world did not really exist for him. The world of his Internal Mother was the only world he knew. But it was a lonely world, devoid of any color and life.

There is still another variation on the need to keep the Internal Parents around and maintain that relationship. Dana explained it very well one day:

> I realized something today that really hit me. I realized today that I've been needing my depression. I've needed the guilt, worthlessness, sadness, and all those feelings that go along with them because they are very intense feelings. When I'm in danger of losing them, I lose very intense feelings and things get very dull, gray, and drab. So when I get those feelings, it's like sticking my finger into an emotional electrical socket and I get all zinged up and I feel alive! It's the same way with my anger at myself and at the world for screwing me up all the time. If I lose that anger towards myself and the world, then I lose a very intense feeling that really makes me feel very alive. That's why I hang on so tightly to those feelings and the thoughts about myself and the world that generate them.

The person who possesses an Inner Other whose basic premise is the valuelessness of the "I" is trapped in a psychological downward spiral. The "I" itself is split and experiences itself as fractured and empty. The irony of it is that the void it experiences is the part of itself that the Inner Other has tricked it into disowning. That experience coincides with the Inner Other's assertion that there is really nothing of any value that resides within the "I."

In an attempt to compensate and fill that void, the Central "I" turns to the Inner Other for its acceptance as a way of filling this deep sense of emptiness. This, however, can never be fulfilled because the very nature of this kind of Internal Parent is to point up and criticize the inadequacies of the "I." It sets up goals and conditions for perfection that a super-person could not attain. But because they are *not* attained, the "I" receives disapproval, criticism, and an enormous amount of guilt for having once again failed the all-important parental figure.

With that as the result of its efforts to heal its internal wounding, the "I" redoubles its efforts to meet the conditions set by the Inner Other. This further widens the split in the "I" which makes the approval all the more imperative. And so on down the spiral.

A break in the spiral can come, however, if the person claims back the Child. That requires that the Inner Other must be disowned. Therein is the leap of faith in the therapeutic process. From the point of view of the person who is bound to the Inner Other through these dynamics, to make that leap seems to be like choosing death. The only way to find that it is not death is to make the leap. That's the catch. The reward is great for the one who does it, though.

Jack: Where's the Little Girl?

Dana: Waiting for her drunken Mother to say something to her. Her Mother doesn't even know she's there.

Jack: Well, who's going to do the mothering here?

Dana: I will do it.

Jack: How are you going to do it? What are you going to say to her? What are you going to do with her?

Dana: I'm trying to lead her away from that stupid drunken bitch. It's hard to pull her away.

Jack: Well, maybe you've got to talk to her a little bit.

Dana: "Come with me. It's better with me. Come away from her. Come with me. [Very quietly and weakly] We have to say goodbye to her."

Jack: How can you have her invest hope in you?

Dana: She's got so much energy expended toward *that woman.*

Jack: That's right.

Dana: She's just bent towards her. Full of tension.

Jack: Maybe you've got to deal with your drunken Mother a little more. What is it you can say to her that the Little Girl cannot?

Dana: [Loudly] "You dumb, stupid bitch. Look at the way you're behaving. Look what you're doing to that Child. You're a bitch! Stupid, drunken, destructive bitch! . . ."

Jack: What is the Child doing?

Dana: She's stopped leaning towards her.

Jack: Why has she stopped leaning?

Dana: Because someone challenged that imbecile woman. And nothing terrible happened. And suddenly the Little Girl realized that that's not the only thing in the whole world to keep the world going.

Jack: Well, talk to the Little Girl now.

Dana: [Quietly but fully] "Come away from her now. She's not strong, she's not strong at all. You don't have to have her. We can have each other and it'll be better. She doesn't mean anything, she's not worth it. Let's not even look back. There's nothing there to see. . . . I'll pay attention." That's such an old scene. I don't remember that I remembered it. My mother never used to come home drunk. One day she came home drunk and she brought me a blackboard. She just palmed it off on me. It was just like a palm-off to keep me out of the way. That whole picture was back in front of my face. And how I felt then. And all this energy has been expended trying to get her attention. I thought I'd burst out of my skin. I just experienced that tension again. Feeling that way again. But now I can claim back that lost part of me and move on!

Once the subject is able to challenge the threat of radical aloneness if it rejects the Inner Other, the manipulations of the Inner Other fall apart. The Self is then left as a unified being with the internal Child occupying its rightful space. Once that happens, there is no room for the presence of the Inner Other. Rather, it disappears and a wholeness of Self takes the place of the fracture.

Finding Others Beyond the Parent

Not only does the Inner Other block the Central "I" from the "Child-I," but it also blocks the "I" from fully experiencing external others. The Inner Other can be so powerful that the Self's experience of external reality is radically altered, so that the subject experiences it as exactly the opposite of what it actually is.

In addition to claiming the Child as a way of releasing oneself from the clutches of the binding and overwhelming Inner Other, working toward hearing and claiming the real response of external persons is also a very powerful tool. Part of that task, of course, is to make sure that a person like Chris or Dana (who either distorts a relationship or searches out others who conform to the inner, denigrating images) finds people who are willing and able to give positive responses.

In the following exchange, Dana is addressing her Internal Mother, who has threatened her with abandonment.

Jack: So what are you going to say to her now? What about her threat of abandonment?

Dana: "See, I don't believe it!" A part of me doesn't believe it because . . . you know what I was just going to say? "I don't believe you're going to leave because you fuckin' need me! And I don't want you to need me!" I wish she would go.

Jack: So, what's the other option?

Dana: "I leave you." Huh. Nice! Very nice. Mmhmm. Mmhmm. "You don't have to go anywhere, 'cause I'm going. Me. I'm going."

Jack: And do you have to be alone in the going?

Dana: Me? No! "See, now when I'm going, I'm not going alone."

Jack: Who are you going with?

Dana: I'm going with everybody I know! [She laughs.] I am.

Jack: Good. Remember that.

Dana: And I'm going to meet more people.

Jack: Great. Remember that. So therefore the threat of abandonment doesn't carry any weight anymore.

Dana: Mmhmm.

Jack: Therefore you can afford to give her up. You can afford to yell back.

Dana: [Sigh.] Yeah. "Oh! Let me let this in."

Jack: Who do you want to say it to? Who's in there you want to say it to?

Dana: To me, I think.

Jack: To the Child. The Child who's afraid of being left alone.
Dana: Yeah.

The beginning of Dana's winning the victory over the tyranny of her Internal Mother came in her feeling the loneliness and identifying it as such. Previously, she would have identified the feeling by simply saying, "I feel anxious," or "I'm feeling upset," or "I'm feeling depressed." In that kind of identification, of course, is a vagueness that did not allow her to get at the source of the feeling.

Anxiety is fear in which the subject cannot identify the violator or the danger. Once we identify the Inner Other and the threats it makes, the anxiety then changes to fear. Once the reasons for the fear are established, we can examine the validity of the fear.

Once Dana was able to identify specifically what the feeling was, she was able to work back to the threat that was coming from inside of her. Then we were able to begin to explore the interaction between herself and her Internal Mother.

Dana needed to reflect on the impact of her Internal Mother's intrusion through her distortion of external reality. Through the contrasting of the new feelings of relief and freedom with the former sense of oppression, loneliness, and anxiety, she was able to realize that these perceptions and feelings did not have to be a fact of life.

Because she previously perceived the Internal Mother as much more powerful than herself, she responded to the violations with fear. This will be clearer if we understand what the difference is between fear and anger. Both anger and fear can be defined as the emotional response to a perception that "I am being violated by someone or something less powerful than I." The only difference between fear and anger is in the perception of the violator. If I am less powerful than the violator, then I must either capitulate to the violator or flee. In anger, however, if I am more powerful, I do not need to capitulate or flee; I can attack so that my boundaries are preserved. Dana could now respond with anger and not fear; that is, she could attack rather than lay herself before her attacker.

Dana had made the mistake of believing that the feelings themselves were the cause of her anguish about her existence.

Feelings, however, do not just happen. They are there because they are the emotional response to some event. Dana's ability to identify the perceptions out of which her feelings flowed was covered up by her unconscious processes. My task in helping her was to assist her to bring into consciousness that which was unconscious.

Interpersonal Retooling

Chris and Dana were trapped within the inner worlds inhabited by their Inner Others and Children and, because of the interaction of these two warring parties, they had come to believe that they couldn't trust the outside world. As children, they had been robbed of their developing ability to process their experience of themselves and others, to weigh and evaluate it, to make judgments about what they were experiencing and then to decide what they would do in response. Not only were they *not* taught and *not* encouraged to learn those kinds of interpersonal skills, they were taught another set of interpersonal skills that were diametrically opposed to them. These skills were: to effectively and efficiently disown their own perceptions about themselves as well as about the outside world; to disown their feeling states; to read as efficiently as possible the non-verbal communications of others that might convey any kind of disapproval of them; and to listen closely to suggestions, directions, and dictums from the Inner Other.

They believed that there was only one kind of interpersonal reality, that everyone was a potential threat because everyone was more powerful than they and therefore would take them over. Their task was to discover that this monolithic view of interpersonal interactions was not entirely accurate. Yes, there are some people out there whose agenda is to take others over and to rule them. This, however, is not everyone's agenda. There are some out there who have no desire to rule others. Rather, they desire to live in peace and harmony, respecting the rights of others and expecting their rights to be respected as well.

Dana and Chris had to learn to give up the politics of their previous interactions. They had to learn to compromise with others, instead of giving in to what they perceived as absolute demands. They had to learn to stop thinking they could read others' minds; instead, they needed to ask what others were thinking and feeling, in order to respond appropriately to them. They had learned as children that compromise was unilateral: they had to bow to any and all demands or requests from the Inner Other without reference to their own needs or desires. Now their task was to discover that their needs and those of the other fell into a hierarchy of importance. The process of mutual compromising is one in which the participants know what their hierarchies are and state them. They then work out together what they can afford to forgo and what they must retain.

For Dana and Chris, attaining these new interpersonal skills was a long process. The results, however, were far more enriching and mutually satisfying than their old ways of relating to others.

11

FLIGHT FROM PAIN

Narcissism

As children, Dana and Chris had been called "selfish" by their parents. These charges continued within them as adults in the persons of their Internal Parents. They were discovering in the course of their psychotherapeutic journey that there is an essential, normal, healthy, and appropriate "selfishness" or narcissism that they needed if they were to have any sense of identity, wholeness, and peace as well as any true connection to the world of outside others.

It is pathological narcissism when the rights of the other or the Self are violated. A part of the maturation task for the child is the growing awareness that the parenting figures, the mother in particular, cannot orient their entire lives around responding to and satisfying the needs of the child. Rather, the parent must teach, and the child must learn, that the parent has limits. There are limits to the extent the parent can respond to the needs of the child (for instance, the parent can't always be present). The parent has needs of its own that do not always coincide with those of the child. If the child does not learn these things, it comes to regard itself as the *only* center in the world around which all other things, personal and impersonal, revolve to satisfy its needs. If this form of pathological narcissism is taught to the child as its state in life, then both it and the world of personal objects that it encounters will continually be violated, abused, and exploited.

The child will be violated because it will develop a deep inner state of loneliness if it cannot recognize others out there with whom it can relate; that is, others with whom there can be an interchange, a give and take, an up-against-ness. Because there is not this up-against-ness, which we have already seen is very necessary and essential in the formation of "I"-identity, the "I" who lives within this pathologically narcissistic framework is denied a fundamental, innate psychological need for the I-thou experience. The emotional response to this kind of object-less experience is loneliness. Others will be habitually, unrecognizably, and usually irreconcilably violated, abused, and exploited, precisely because this kind of person was never taught the reality and meaning of another's boundaries.

By way of contrast, normal, appropriate, necessary narcissism begins with the assumption that the subject is the center of its awareness to which no one else has access. No one else can determine what the subject needs, feels, thinks unless it chooses through language or some other communication to reveal those inner states to the other. In that sense knowing itself as the center of itself is absolute.

But the same subject also recognizes there are other "I's" out there who are the centers of their own personal, self-conscious inner worlds and as such are absolute and incontestable authorities about those inner, personal worlds. Two self-aware subjects who meet may choose to reveal their inner selves to each other. If two (or more) people choose to reveal and share those inner realities, that is choosing to move toward intimacy. Not sharing is a choice (conscious or unconscious) of nonintimacy—a choice anyone has a right to make. If anyone is to be satisfied psychologically in the interpersonal encounter, the basic, underlying reason for the encounter must be to reveal who I am and to find out who you are. In that is the life-giving stimulation that generates the state of personal self-awareness—I-am-who-I-am. As I am revealing who I am, not only do I discover aspects or facets of my existence (happiness, joy, an idea, event, or whatever), but the act itself is stimulating, which brings me to self-awareness. Conversely, as I listen to who the other is, not only do I learn the particulars about the other, but in the act of listening itself, I am stimulated and come again to a state of self-awareness. That is the scintillation and life-giving quality of the interpersonal event we all so urgently yearn after.

Dana and Chris were taught a third form of narcissism: a narcissism based on the disowning of the "I" needs and substituting responding to the needs of others. In their case, the

Other—the Parent—was the authority who told them who they were and what the world was. Further, their purpose in life was to take care of the world and to devalue their needs so that the Other would always be primary in all things.

If they did not comply with this view, they were threatened or punished physically or psychologically by the all-important Other. To avoid especially the psychological pain of the sentence—loneliness for Dana or loss of identity for Chris—they incorporated the internal images of the parental prohibitions to stop them from claiming their normal, narcissistic perspective of themselves-in-the-world. Others in the world were for them nothing more than "ideas" that were formulated by their Inner Other with little or no input on the part of the real outside other. Any experience of another human being was not the experience of a true other but a mirage created by the Inner Other. They were unable to acknowledge the real other as existing beyond the confines of their own inner processes.

On the one hand, Dana was obsessed about being rejected by the Other if she didn't conform to the inner agenda established by her Inner Others. Because of that, she was not concerned with the other person; that is, hearing the other reveal itself to her or respond to its needs. Rather, she was preoccupied with saving herself from what she thought was the insurmountable pain of experience if she should be rejected by the other, as predicted by her Inner Other. Chris, on the other hand, was obsessed with the idea of being overwhelmed by the other. As long as he listened to his Internal Mother, he could not discover the real other. Because he was so preoccupied with the possible overwhelming event, he could not establish any interpersonal ties. In either instance, both appeared to be preoccupied about their others, but that, too, was a mirage. They were really concerned about preserving themselves from imagined pain. The irony was that, to avoid the parental charges of "selfishness," they appeared to be other-directed. In reality, though, they were self-obsessed.

Guilt

All of the people I have worked with in my counseling practice have been marked by a profound, deep, pervasive feeling of guilt about their very existence. This underlying sense of guilt, whether it is expressed and dealt with in theological, artistic, or psychological terms, is a very powerful one and is present in most human thought and endeavor, whether personal, familial, educational, ecclesiastical, or political. The dynamic of the Inner Other versus the Self has raised the problem of what guilt is and, further, why people in general feel so guilty about their existences. But just as the psycho-therapeutic process has raised the question, it has also provided some of the answers.

Guilt, as a subjective experience, is a feeling state: an emotional response to a perception on the part of the subject that it has, in some way, violated another and thereby is vulnerable to a punishment. This is in contradistinction to an objective fact of guilt: that is, that the rights or boundaries of another have, in fact, been violated by the subject. The reality of the wrongdoing is present whether or not the subject responds emotionally to the fact of the wrongdoing or the possibility of punishment. The feeling, then, informs the human organism of its possible vulnerability to a punishment (whatever form that may take). The feeling state, in turn, is the first step in arousing the organism to prepare for the possible punishment.

So guilt—a reality which many of us fail to understand and which causes us a great deal of internal turbulence when it need not—falls into two categories. The first kind of guilt is real or actual guilt. The feeling is a response to an actual event, in which the rights of another have really been violated. The second kind of guilt is what I call psychological guilt. It is an emotional state of disturbance, usually chronic, in which there is an awareness of having committed some more or less terrible wrongdoing or "sin" which is rather nebulous and undefinable. In this disturbance, the Self continues to receive the communication that it is a being devoid of any worth and in some way responsible for that worthlessness and emptiness.

For example, how often have we heard parents say to a child, "What? You're doing badly in math? How could you do this to me?" Rather than looking on that kind of event as the child's problem with which it needs help, the parent adds an insurmountable problem—namely, the child's failure to the parent—to the already existing one. The child thus comes to believe that it is intrinsically inadequate as a person and that it is not responsible to itself but only to the Other—"I don't do and learn math for myself but for my parent(s)." The failure to do and learn math, then, is a failure, not to the Self but to the Other.

With that, the subject comes to believe it is responsible for the Other's agenda and feelings regarding it. Any failure to meet up to the Other's expectation is a failure and violation of the other. The child comes to believe that it is responsible for fulfilling the Other's expectations of it no matter what they are. Any failure to do that renders the subject profoundly guilty.

The child's belief that it must give anything and everything the Other demands of it or face enormous guilt and some sort of terrible punishment lives on into adulthood in the interaction between Internal Other and the Self. Dana heard this kind of expectation when she had the party and the voice was saying: "You have to circulate. You have to be pleasant. You've got to take care of everyone. Don't think about yourself. If you start thinking about yourself, you will fail your guests. Then you will be guilty." Chris heard it when his Internal Mother said to him: "You've nothing to give to anyone. You're just garbage. So don't get involved because they'll find out how inadequate you are. You will fail them and then you'll really feel guilty, so stay away!" Any failure to fulfill all expectations the Other had of them resulted in unbearable guilt. They then established patterns, each in their own way, to side-step this responsibility—patterns which imprisoned them in a never-ending merry-go-round of conflicts and unresolved attempts to escape.

As long as the subject continues to believe in the underlying assumption of its absolute responsibility to fulfill the needs of the Other if it is to have any worth, it remains enslaved by the Inner Other. Its real incapacity to live up to those most unreal and monumental internal expectations feeds its all-pervasive sense of emptiness. Its belief in its incapacity to respond to these rigid and impossible demands is a testimony to and judgment of its fundamental guilt toward the Other. It finds itself inextricably caught in the web of its guilt and punishment so that, no matter which way it moves, it risks either the loss of the Other or the loss of its identity.

Dana attempted to dodge the sense of guilt for her inadequacy, worthlessness, emptiness, etc., by avoiding decision-making altogether. She unconsciously reasoned that if she could avoid making a decision, she could avoid any internal charges that she had made the wrong one. She avoided decision-making in two ways, either by not making any decisions at all (which resulted in immobility) or by manipulating others into making them for her. This way of handling the problem, however, had a boomerang effect and a punishment of its own. She did lower the level of the negative judgments against herself, but, in so doing, she had to contend with the terrible psychological pain contained in her loss of self-identity. No matter which way she moved, she was trapped in terrible pain: either loss of identity or loss of the other and resultant guilt about her very existence. It was not a pleasant dilemma to be in!

Chris found another device by which he thought he could sidestep the issue of his worthlessness, inadequacy, and the guilt for that. By avoiding involvement with anyone, he avoided having to live up to the expectations of Others. "If there aren't others around to have expectations of me," he reasoned unconsciously, "then I can't fail them. If I'm not failing, I'm not guilty." He failed to realize that it wasn't the outside world that had all these expectations of him, but rather the maternal demon that rattled around inside. In so isolating himself from others, he thought he minimalized his sense of guilt for his "inadequacies." There was a basis in reality for this belief, for as long as he kept himself isolated, his Internal Mother was more or less quiescent because there was little for her to criticize. When his loneliness became unbearable and he would wander out to seek even the most minimal form of companionship by tentatively engaging some external other, his Internal Mother would be aroused from her lair and hit him with charges of worthlessness about his inadequacy to fulfill the needs of the other. To absolve himself from the guilt of these charges and protect himself from the attacker (who he thought was the outside person), he retreated to his thick-walled but very lonely castle to wait for another chance to surreptitiously slip out once more to ease the pain of the loneliness.

Relating Through Guilt

One of the fundamental assumptions Dana and Chris granted to the Inner Others was that they existed and therefore lived according to other people's reasons and judgments. Any failure to do this, no matter how insignificant, rendered them guilty of having failed the Other and of being worthless as persons by the judgment of these internal lawmakers. Whenever they made any attempt at coming to know themselves through their feelings, needs, wants, and thoughts, they were faced with the internal charges of: "How dare you think about yourself! What a selfish person you are to think *only* of yourself!" (The emphasis on the *only* by the Internal Other comes out of the assumption that every subjective ounce of energy must be spent on responding to the Other.) "They (the world) will find out how selfish you are. And because you are selfish (incapable of loving), they will discover and judge you to be a 'bad' person (empty and worthless). They then will reject you (punishment) for being the 'bad' person you are. So if you give up thinking about yourself (your needs, feelings, thoughts, perceptions, and judgments) and rely on the Other (its needs, feelings, thoughts, perceptions, and judgments), maybe they won't reject you and everything will be OK."

Dana and Chris heard the Inner Other saying something like this: "If you love me, you will give me anything and everything I ask of you, including your self-identity. If you are unwilling to give me everything, you don't love me. If you don't love me (give me everything I ask of you), you have failed me. If you don't love me, you don't have any worth or value as a person. If you don't have worth or value, I will reject you." Within that definition of love, it turns out that L-O-V-E is really spelled G-U-I-L-T. Rather than relating through an experience of warmth, affection, trust, mutuality, and intimacy, the victims of this Inner Other relate through an anticipation of the violation of the Other because of the impossibility of conforming to the above definition of love. The Central "I" finds itself either immersed in a profound sense of guilt or constantly immersed in maneuvering to avoid the sense of guilt by conforming to the demands and expectations the Other appears to have. Contained in that syndrome of guilt is worthlessness, helplessness, inner void, self-hate, and endless anxiety.

The engagement of two (or more) people who accept this system as their relational operating principle can be expressed through a series of equations. Remember that (within this way of perceiving relatedness) the Other demands that "I" absolutely take care of it and, in turn, the Other will tell "me" who I am in my feelings, needs, thoughts, etc., and in so doing give me my very life through providing me with identity. The equation becomes:

(1) I give myself to you.	=	You give yourself over to me.
	or	
(2) I become responsible for you.	=	You become responsible for me.
	or	
(3) I take care of you.	=	You take care of me.
	or	
(4) I guess what your feelings, needs, wants, thoughts, judgments are.	=	You guess what my feelings, needs, wants, thoughts, judgments are.

Dana was very much in conformity to these equations when she spoke of Bob after the visit to the doctor's office. "He should have known that I wanted to say something (#4). . . . I feel so guilty for having wanted him to shut up because he would have been 'hurt' by my need to speak (#2) and let me speak." Within this guilt system of "loving," Dana had committed the terrible sin of feeling angry because *she* had a need to speak to the doctor herself. Within that framework, she would have "pushed" Bob aside. To push him aside was a violation of Bob for which she was now profoundly guilty. The only way she could repair the damage of her "violation" of Bob, her act of "unlove," and her guilt for that was to steel herself even more adamantly against herself, to disown herself all the more by locking her lips all the more tightly. But, as she did that, she disappeared even more radically, which was the ultimate violation—against herself.

Chris, too, operated within the structure of the same equations. Implicit in his long absence from the group was, "You should have known I was having trouble (failure on our part to live up to #3) and told me what to do (#2)." This was also implied in his statement, "I didn't really think I was important enough (the other is always more important) so that you would understand." In the fact of our not understanding (because he had not revealed or told anything to us beyond the fact of his absence), we had failed him in "love" because we had not followed and therefore failed in equation #4. Since we hadn't conformed to that rule, he believed at a preconscious level that we had violated him. A part of his absence was unconsciously intended as a punishment: he withdrew his love from us because we had failed him.

In this sort of relationship, "loving" the other includes knowing what the other is thinking, feeling, wanting, knowing, perceiving, judging, without the other ever stating in any direct, verbal way what its internal states are. The only evidence the subject has to go on are indefinite, nonverbal, bodily signals. Because of internal pressure, people like Dana and Chris had come to believe that nonverbal signals were as accurate and precise as language in communicating the internal states of the Other. They thus drew conclusions about the internal states of Others (that were often not warranted) and then treated these hypotheses about the Other as a fact of existence about them.

One day in discussing Dana's tendency to do this and her inability to comprehend why she could not use bodily cues to determine precisely the inner state of the Other, I was aware that my arms were tightly folded around my body and my knees were drawn up as well. *The* reason, *my* reasons, for my body being in that posture was that the office was cold that day (at least to me) and I was trying to conserve my body heat. I wondered, though, how *she* was interpreting my bodily posture. So I asked her. She said, "You're angry with me because I didn't understand what you were talking about." I responded, "Yes, I am feeling something—you are right about that. But your statement of *what* I am feeling is not accurate. I am feeling physically cold, not angry." There was a look of surprise on her face and then a sigh. I *hypothesized* that the sigh meant relief, but I asked her what it meant. She did confirm that it was relief—from the anxiety that had begun, subconsciously, to build up as a result of her guess which had become a fact for her, namely, my anger. She began to realize what she did to herself as well as to me in the mind reading. It finally dawned on her that her mind reading of the internal states of others through these nonspecific forms of communication was invalid, caused her great harm, and did a great disservice to the Other.

The objective reality is that there is no way I can know what precisely is happening inside the Other unless the Other tells me. Anything short of that is a guess and only a guess.

Although there is a gross error in judging what the subjective state of the Other is because of false assumptions and beliefs about the Self and the Other, this does not diminish the relatedness of the subject to the Other. On the contrary, there is an intense perceptual as well as emotional response to the Other, especially if the Other is also operating within the context of these same beliefs. The emotional glue of this kind of relating is the binding of two people through the sense of guilt generated in failing the Other or the anxiety about the possibility of failure. Both these feelings are very powerful ones and, therefore, can create intense bonds between persons.

Although these feelings are very unpleasant and painful, they nevertheless are very powerful and, thereby, very stimulating. In lieu of anything else (self-worth, mutuality with the other, etc.), the subject seeks out these feelings and even strives to reenforce them within the relational event. To give up these stimulation states is to give up the chance of stimulation *per se*. There is little or nothing else contained for the subject in the interpersonal event beyond the sense of worthlessness, failure toward the other, and ultimately the guilt because the Inner Other has blocked any other kind of Other-experience. The prospect of being stimulated in the engagement with the Other in self-worth, mutuality, warmth, trust, etc., is totally foreign. To give up the guilt then confronts the subject with the spectre of absolute nothingness.

On the other hand, as stimulation states, they are intensely stimulating and thereby very enlivening. Therefore, at one and the same time, as the subject tries to run from the painful sense of guilt and worthlessness in the relational event, it also attempts to foster and reenforce them. This is what Dana was referring to when she talked about her depression being like the zing of an electrical shock. At the root of her depression was the all-pervasive sense of guilt, which, if she could "plug" into it, would make her again feel alive!

There is another side to this process, however. One side of the guilt-love contract is the loss of self-identity and power. The other side, though, is taking responsibility for and exercising power over the Other. The subject can vicariously fill up a part of the void left by the abdication of its responsibility and power over its own existence. If I can't have power and control over my own existence and therefore a sense of substance about myself, I can fill up that void by secondarily becoming responsible for and exercising power and control over the Other. This, then, is another way in which the Other "gives" worth and substance to the subject. This, of course, is why people who are entrapped in this belief system hold so tenaciously onto being responsible for others yet are unable to function for themselves. Dana lived this out when she protected Bob from "hurt" when she kept her mouth shut during the doctor's visit. She was exercising power over his feeling states by guessing what they would in fact be and protecting him from those "guessed" feeling states by not doing something she needed to do, i.e., request him to be silent during the interview. She assumed responsibility for his feeling states because she believed she would be guilty of his "hurt" if she spoke. Therefore, she didn't speak. But the other side of that was her deep need to run his life this way, because in the very act of voiding herself she gained some of herself back by vicariously becoming Bob.

Not only do the subjects have an investment in maintaining their own sense of guilt in their relatedness to the Other, they also have an investment in maintaining the sense of guilt in the Other. If the one relinquishes its belief that it is responsible for the Other, it also relinquishes the guilt if it does not conform. It will not allow the subject to assume power and control over it.

The subject is then radically confronted with its own void, for which it can no longer compensate in that relationship. That can be a very disturbing and overwhelming experience for the subject so invested.

This whole system, then, places an impossible burden on both the subject and the Other. In the relationship, the expectation is that I have more knowledge about the Other than I have of myself. Similarly, the Other is expected to have more knowledge about me than I have of myself. The equation then becomes: I am responsible for the whole world (minus one person, me) = The whole world is responsible for me (minus one person, me).

If I accept the conditions in this equation—that I must know what is happening inside the Other before the Other articulates it or knows what that is itself—then I also bear the burden of a task that is impossible to perform: one hundred percent accuracy at guessing the inside state of the other.

By the same token, if the world fails to guess my needs, it has failed me. Since I cannot claim, by definition, any substance of my own, the world has failed me by failing to fill my inner emptiness. Since the rule of one hundred percent accuracy applies to both sides of the equation, the world is always in danger of failing me. The world of others thus cannot be trusted because it, at times, fails to fill that terrible sense of inner void.

If we take a closer look at the equation, we can see how deep that sense of void really is. The burden of the whole world rests upon someone who is not there. The internal other tells the "I" it must give up itself in deference to the other. The "I" places the other into the void created by its disappearance.

On the other side of the equation, the world is responsible for defining someone who isn't there, who, in a sense, doesn't exist. Thus, no matter how the world might respond to the "I" it doesn't make any difference what the response is because the "I" isn't there.

Because the "I" does not appear on either side of the equation, there is no point from which the "I" can respond or be responded to. There is just an empty void that is, at best, filled with the presence of the Inner Other telling the Central "I" who it and the world are. At no point does it or the world of others exist in relation to it. The "I" becomes a mirage to itself, in its response to Others and Others responding to it.

There is another way of viewing the Self and the world, however. It runs as follows: (1) I am the only person who knows what is going on inside of me and the Other is the only one who knows what is going on inside itself; (2) I have the responsibility to articulate that to myself as well as the Other and the Other has the responsibility to articulate that to itself and to me and the rest of the world. (3) I have power over my life; the Other has power over itself. When we meet and interact, the contract of that interaction is one in which we each state who we are. As I's focused and centered from the primary experience of ourselves, we each are grounded from a reference point that is indisputable. We accept responsibility for something that is within our grasp, that is reasonable and our right and responsibility, namely, ourselves.

If this is the basis within which two or more people agree to relate, then the old neurotic equation becomes a new order of self-health. I am responsible for myself = you are responsible for yourself. When I engage the Other, I am not preoccupied with preserving myself from disappearing in the Other because that is not the threat. I am guaranteed that I remain who I am because the very basis of the interaction is the agreement that I am the only person who knows who I am, and that is what is respected.

With this as the operating principle I violate neither myself nor the Other. I do not violate myself because I am affirming myself as I draw from the experience of myself as I relate to the Other. I do not violate the Other because, as I stand in my own center, I have the only base I can have, myself, from which I can truly see and hear who the Other truly is. I do not violate the Other by relating to that person out of an image that I created out of thoughts that begin and end in my own head. I am able to experience the reality of that person. I am able to listen without contamination from my own assumptions.

Therefore each of us can listen to the Other. Once we have heard each other, we can weigh all the information that we have about the Other. If we need more, we can ask for it so that we do not make assumptions whose only reality is based in our own thoughts. Once we have done that, we can respond to each other, within the limitations of who each of us is at that moment.

12

NEW TOOLS TOWARD SELF-OBSERVATION

The History

As sentient, self-aware beings, we possess a whole array of mechanisms which help us to preserve our lives, physically and psychologically. As we move from the helpless and radically dependent state of infancy into childhood, through childhood to adolescence and finally adulthood, there is a progression by which these mechanisms become more complex. As they become more complex, there is a psycho-biological design which should help us better to cope, survive, and indeed live in a world in which we are productive and creative, have mastery over ourselves as well as aspects of our environment, and live in relative harmony within ourselves and with others.

Parts of this psycho-biological maturation include a growing awareness of feeling states, an ability to separate the Self-reality from the Other-reality, to weigh and evaluate the experience of Self as well as the experience of others, and to arrive at judgments about those experiences of Self and Others. This is ideally what should have happened. Frequently, however, it did *not* happen.

An essential part of this psycho-biological maturation process is the required presence of parental figures who acted as models. Although the abilities to feel, to process experience, and to arrive at judgments are capabilities intrinsic to the human organism, unless they are tapped at their appropriate developmental times through contact with others (socialization), they will either not be available to the human person at all, or they will be developed in stunted or dysfunctional ways. By way of a parallel example, we know that a child reaches a point in its cognitive, developmental history when the ability to learn to read or do arithmetic appears; but if that ability is not addressed, tapped, and developed during that period, it may never develop or is at least severely curtailed or limited. So, too, it is with these other psycho-social capabilities. And not only must these abilities be addressed at the right time, they must be modeled in the right way. Unfortunately, they often are not. To understand our current predicaments, therefore, it is necessary to understand the flawed developmental process we may have been exposed to.

Feelings

As sentient, self-aware beings, we possess a variety of possible feeling states that inform us about the state of things inside or outside of ourselves. These fall into two major categories. Some feelings inform the organism that all is not well: either the physical or the psychological aspects of its well-being are endangered. Such psychological danger would be, for instance, loss of identity, loss of autonomy, or loss or lowering of stimulation states—all of which could lead to a loss of self-awareness. This category of feeling states I label as "warning feelings." Many people label them as "negative feelings." This is not a helpful label, for the word "negative" connotes a meaning of "unwanted." As we shall see, they are important and needed states to possess and recognize. The other major category of feelings are those that inform the human organism that "all is well," that the organism is in a state of positive homeostasis, well-being. This group I label "feelings of well-being."

Warning	*Well-being*
Anger	Wholesomeness
Fear	Peace
Anxiety	Joy
Frustration	Excitement
Disappointment	Happiness
Sadness	Playfulness
Loneliness	Warmth
Boredom	Affection
Confusion	Connectedness
Guilt	etc.
etc.	

I would like to define some of the warning feelings more specifically:

Anger, Fear, Anxiety—The responses to some outside threat or violation to the physical or psychological boundaries of the person.
Frustration—The response when a goal the subject has striven to attain is blocked.
Disappointment—The response when an event anticipated by the subject does not happen.
Sadness—The response when there is the loss of the stimulation of a significant Other.
Loneliness—The response when the stimulation of interpersonal contact falls below that which is needed to maintain the self-aware state.
Boredom—The response when the general stimulation state begins to drop to levels at which self-awareness is in jeopardy.
Confusion—The response when the Self, boundaries, goals, purposes, concepts, etc., fade and become indistinct.
Guilt—The response to the anticipated loss of the Other as a source of stimulation resulting from a wrongdoing by the subject toward the Other because of a rupture of the connectedness between the subject and the Other.

To understand what happens when a feeling or group of feelings is disowned, let's examine the subcategory of "threat" feelings, namely anger and fear. Anger is an emotional response to a perception that there is a violator of the physical or psychological person of the subject, and the subject perceives itself as equal to or more powerful than the intruder or violator. In fear, the subject perceives itself as less powerful than the violator and is therefore at the mercy of the violator.

The feeling, whether anger or fear, mobilizes the subject to take action to preserve itself. On the occasion of fear, the organism is mobilized either to flee or to submit to the more powerful violator. In the latter choice, submission, the subject hopes and often pleads for mercy from the violator in the hope it will not attack. In anger, however, the mobilization and response is different. Rather than fleeing or submitting, the subject is mobilized either to stand its ground before the attacker or to attack back.

Obviously, how people are *taught* to respond to feelings like anger or fear and how they are *taught* to perceive the violator are going to determine to a large extent how they *will* respond. If a child was taught (as many of us were) to disown its anger, the child was taught to render itself helpless and defenseless before others. This is so because, if the anger is disowned, the subject also disowns the capability of perceiving itself as being at least the equal of its adversaries. With that, it loses the capability of defending itself against any kind of intrusion or attack. Without anger, the human organism loses any possibility for self-defense. With the loss of anger as a response to reality, the only emotional alternative the subject has in reaction to a violation is fear: the only perspective the subject can have is perceiving itself as weaker and at the mercy of the Other. The only action that is left in response to a violation is either fleeing (Chris) or submission (Dana).

As time elapses, the subject "forgets" its original reasons for the fear, because of the cloudiness of childhood itself and because of the very unresolvability of the fear. Now the feeling becomes a response to the threat of a threat. The threat of a threat is an inability to defend oneself against any potential violation by another. Any person or event becomes a threat because the subject finds itself helpless before anyone. This is when the fear fades into anxiety. Fear is the emotional response to a specific violator who appears to be more powerful than the subject. Anxiety occurs when there is a perception of a violation, but the violator cannot be specified. Because of the insubstantial ground of anxiety, it tends to feed upon itself until it becomes monumental and out of control. The more it mushrooms, the more the subject believes it to be self-generating.

This is when the subject falls into a trap laid by the Inner Others. There is no feeling that is self-generated. All feelings are in response to some event, whether inside or outside the Self experienced by the subject. However, because the subject has been taught not to respond to "threat" feelings, they appear to be self-generating. Because of that belief, they *do* get out of control.

The interaction to which the subject is responding lies within the unconscious realm of the psyche. Because the unconscious *is* unconscious, the subject has little or no access to these internal processes. Although this part of ourselves is unavailable to our conscious consideration, it is, nevertheless, one of two realities in which we exist. And, in fact, it is a reality in which we are often intensely engaged and by which we are very much influenced, a reality in which the subject is engaged in intense, emotional responses between itself as Central "I" and "Child-I" and the internal object-persons.

The only hope any one of us has to bring about any sense of resolution and peace to the Self is to drag these unconscious personae and their processes and our responses to them out into the open light of consciousness so that the heretofore unknown threat can become known and addressed in some way. The following is a session with Dana in which she begins with her all-pervasive sense of anxiety and what happened when she was able to touch into the internal and very real processes that she in fact was responding to with the anxiety:

Jack: Well, how are you today?
Dana: I'm very anxious.
Jack: What are you anxious about?
Dana: I'm just anxious.
Jack: Well, the anxiety is in response to something. What goes on inside of you when you experience the anxiety?
Dana: I feel that I can't get out of this anxiety.
Jack: Well, that's not a feeling. What do you feel when you think that you can't get out of the anxiety?
Dana: Anxious.
Jack: Ah. So you're feeling anxious about being anxious?
Dana: Yes.
Jack: Well, let's take a look at that. What are the thoughts you have when you think you can't get out of the anxiety? Can you quote them?
Dana: I say to myself, "You're never going to get out of this. You're too weak to cope with all this anxiety." When that happens, I don't know what to do.

Jack: Did you hear the "you"?
Dana: Yes! It's them talking again!
Jack: They sure are. Let's take a look at what they're saying.
Dana: They say, "You won't know what to do with all this anxiety. You're too weak to do anything about it. You just can't cope with anything."
Jack: Well, is that true that you can't cope with anything? What about getting here today? It was difficult, wasn't it?
Dana: Yes.
Jack: But you made it, right? That means that you coped, doesn't it?
Dana: Yeah, it does.
Jack: So what does that do to their premise that you can't cope, that you are always at their mercy?
Dana: Well, it's not true!
Jack: They're lying to you again, aren't they?
Dana: Yeah.
Jack: Well, how do you feel about that?
Dana: Well, I'm afraid I can't do anything about that.
Jack: You can't do anything about what?
Dana: About the anxiety.
Jack: I'm not so sure about that. The anxiety is a response to a threat that is unspecified. But we've discovered the threat, haven't we? Them.
Dana: Yeah.
Jack: So now you're afraid—afraid you can't do anything about them—right?
Dana: Yeah, I feel so weak.
Jack: Who's robbing you of your strength?
Dana: Well, they are!
Jack: Well, what do you want to say to them for robbing you of your strength? How do you feel toward them for doing that?
Dana: Angry. I hate it when I feel this way.
Jack: Well, what do you want to say to them for lying to you and deceiving you into believing that you are helpless before them, that you are at their mercy, and that you have to suffer this terrible, endless anxiety when they are around? What do you want to do to them? [While I have been saying this, I have moved the parental bag so that it stands next to her chair and leans over her shoulder.]
Dana: "Get away from me!" [She pushes the bag away and gets up to punch and kick it.] "All you do is lie and cheat me! I'm

sick and tired of you! I'm going to kick you out, you bastards! Go to hell." [She returns to her chair a little out of breath, looking much more alive than she had before.]

Jack: Well, how do you feel now?

Dana: Relieved! Much more alive. I was feeling so drained before with the anxiety.

Jack: Where is the anxiety?

Dana: Gone!

Jack: That's right. Does that say anything to you?

Dana: Yeah. The anxiety is caused by them and if I can figure out what they are doing, I can get rid of the anxiety.

This, of course, is where psychotherapy can be helpful in revealing the underlying unconscious processes that generate the spiraling anxiety, not only to address specific states of anxiety but also to assist the person to discover ways in which it can monitor and address these same, ongoing unconscious processes itself. The eventual goal is to train someone like Dana to develop a finely tuned ability to observe herself, to be able to read the "language" of the unconscious, so that she will be able to do by herself what I helped her do in this session.

Initially, though, the subject, who is at the mercy of these unconscious relationships and interactions, is not aware of the unconscious language and processes. Because the underlying assumptions to which the subject has capitulated over the years are so habitual, it does not notice the leaps in logic that it takes which keep the system going.

However, to an outside observer, especially to one who is trained to look for and understand these kinds of leaps, they can be quite glaring. The task for the skilled observer and questioner is to engage the subject. As we challenge doggedly, one by one, the leaps in logic, unveil the real logic of the internal others, look at their beginning assumptions, and discover their falsity and the feelings generated once the false assumptions are granted to the Inner Other, new, truer starting assumptions can be established and *different* feelings generated.

Both Dana and Chris discovered and built on this type of experience in the course of their therapeutic journey. Dana found out she did not have to cringe before these powerful Inner Others. Rather, the more she exercised the power of her anger against them, the more powerless they were rendered. Likewise, Chris found he no longer had to flee others as reincarnations of his vicious Internal Mother. Rather he could stand his ground, challenge her attempts at isolating him from the outside world of others and discover that they were not, in fact, mere extensions of her.

Conflicts around feelings states are not always a function of the intended prohibition on the part of the parental figure. Sometimes there are conditions within the family in which the child finds itself inextricably trapped. It experiences feelings for which there seems to be no outlet or resolution. The only solution left to the child seems to be to deny the fact of the feelings because the mere pain of them makes it difficult to cope. The child, then, enters into a kind of psychological anesthetization of these painful feeling states.

Let us say, as an example, that a child has a mother who is chronically depressed. When the child feels lonely and asks the mother for stimulation, she does not respond adequately. The child is therefore left with feelings of loneliness which it cannot resolve. It may then learn to use food to anesthetize its feelings of loneliness.

Again, through the psycho-therapeutic process, the layers can be stripped away so that the real focus of the pain can be addressed. Jon, who was working on this deep-seated issue of loneliness, described standing at the refrigerator door looking for something to eat after having just eaten a rather substantial meal. As he stood there gazing into the lighted refrigerator, not too sure what he was looking for, he began to question why he was there in the first place. He decided that he could not possibly be hungry since he had just eaten. Yet he had this deep and terrible yearning for *something*.

He closed the refrigerator door and began to converse with his inner Child. At that point, the clear answer from inside came that the yearning was born out of loneliness. He thought of ways in which he could respond to the need. He called a friend and told him what had just happened. When he did this, the deep, painful yearning melted away, and for the first time in a long time he felt at peace with himself and satisfied at a level that he rarely felt after eating.

This coincided with a part of his developmental history which included a mother who was chronically depressed and therefore largely unavailable to Jon. Meal times were the time of the day when the family had some interaction; the mother's depression was diluted by the presence of the other family members, and Jon's loneliness lifted somewhat. Further, Jon remembered getting positive affirmation and attention for eating, as he had been a light eater as a child. Because of this context, Jon learned to associate food with the lessening of the pain of his loneliness as a child.

With these insights and experience, he was more and more able to understand and deal constructively with his compulsive eating habits. Gradually, the pervasive sense of hunger for food began to subside; he became more aware of the loneliness, painful though it was. But as he addressed each awareness of the loneliness and *did something about it,* the intensity of the loneliness diminished so that it finally became a reasonable feeling response to a real situation—namely, at times he needed interaction with others because he by virtue of circumstance was alone, not because he had been trapped in the aloneness in his childhood.

Watching the Language

In addition to understanding the significance of feelings, there is another category of expression that can be a tool helping the subject to gain power over the Inner Others and heal the rift that exists between the Central "I" and "Child-I." This category is language which can help us to understand the significance of words and how they can either support the Inner Others in their control of the Self or be used to support self-identity, autonomy, and integrity.

The child that found itself subject to an overpowering parental figure learned to use a vocabulary and grammar that helped it incorporate the image of that parent and to disown or hide the parts of itself that proved to be unacceptable to the parent. It is this same kind of vocabulary and grammar in the adult that keeps this Inner Other in a position of domineering power over the Central "I" and keeps it separated from the "Child-I."

On the other hand, there is another language, diametrically opposed in grammar and vocabulary to the internal parental language, that affirms and reinforces the "I" and undermines the seemingly indisputable authority of it. To achieve independence from the rule of Inner Other authority, we must know that there is, in fact, an intense internal conversation and that two different languages exist—languages that can be used within the context of this conversation.

As we have seen, one of the most familiar words of the parental language is the word "you." The subject believes that it is addressing itself when this "you" form of language is used. In fact, however, the subject is being addressed by the Inner Other. Whether the Inner Other is engaging the Central "I" in an outright attack or appears to be offering it some "sage" advice, the subject is being undermined by the activity of the Inner Other.

However, once the subject becomes aware of the psychological importance of these verbal slippages, it can watch for them. When they occur, the subject can then learn to examine their meaning and impact on itself and to address the now overt activity of the Inner Other. A part of that process is to substitute "I" where there was previously "you," and to examine the emotional impact of the replacement of words as well as the change in meaning of the sentence. More often than not, there is a profound change at both the emotional and cognitive levels. The subject can then begin addressing the Inner Other with all the anger that needs to be expressed for its intrusions and violations of the Self.

The knowledge of the significance of the "you" address is not enough, however, to free someone from the slavery of it. That knowledge is only the beginning. To be free, the subject must be willing to battle this inner voice. If the subject backs off from this confrontation for fear of the apparent consequences, then the oppression and slavery will continue.

In addition to the outright "you" address there is another, more subtle use of "you" language behind which the Inner Other lurks. It is what I call the dissociative use of "you." It usually happens when a person is describing something it experienced to someone else. Rather than using "I" and "my," the person uses "you" and "your." An example of this dissociative use of "you" would be the following: "I was having a good time at my party last week. But then John came up and told me, 'You should be taking care of the guests instead of standing around talking to everyone.' You know how angry you get when someone like John comes along and tells you how to run your life."

Here, the subject is not being addressed by some inner voice. Rather, it is attempting to displace its anger with John onto the listener: "You know how angry you get. . . ." In fact, it is not the listener's event with John, it is the speaker's. The proposition the speaker is making, though, is that it *is* the listener's event. When I hear someone with whom I am working enter into a similar shift, I replay the tape and have the person replace the inappropriate "you's" with appropriate "I's." It is even possible to experience a shift in meaning and feeling repeating something that is fairly neutral to the subject. In order to understand how this shift can occur, I would suggest that you go back to the original descriptive example and repeat it out loud to yourself as though you were the original speaker of it. After you have done that, repeat it, but this time change it to: "I was having a good time at my party last week. But then John came up and told me, 'You should be taking care of the guests instead of standing around talking to everyone.' I really get angry when someone like John comes along and tells me how to run my life."

When I go through this kind of self-observation exercise with someone I'm working with, there is a fairly universal response. When I ask what happened to the anger in the "you" form of the description, the person describes and points to the anger as being "out there," somewhere indefinite in the middle of the room. However, when asked where the anger is when "I" was substituted, the person usually points to the Self, frequently the breast. When asked about the experience, they describe in one way or another a sense of solidity, centeredness, and power about the Self. Much of the time, the "you" form is described as being one of insubstantiality about the Self, little or no feeling of anger, and an overall sense of powerlessness. As people become more aware of this dissociative use of "you" and change it to the first person when they are describing a truly personal event, they discover they begin to form a deeper sense of Self.

Another dissociative phrase that is used very frequently with very similar effects is the phrase, "I feel that. . . ." Most of the time when people use this phrase, they come out with a thought statement, not a feeling. An example of this is: "I feel that I am taking too much time in the group tonight." The person who might use this sentence may have feelings, some of them very intense, that accompany the thought and therefore the perception. Therefore, when I hear this type of sentence being used, the interaction is typically as follows:

Jack: You *think* you are taking too much time with the group. What are you feeling, thinking you are taking too much time?
Response: I feel (anxious, guilty, uncomfortable, etc.)

When the speaker uses such a dissociative phrase, the listener is prepared for information that is not forthcoming. This can be confusing. And when I ask the speaker whether he or she was aware of the feeling that finally became articulated in the interaction, the answer often is, "No, I really couldn't and didn't identify the feeling until you asked me the question." Therefore, not only the listener is baffled and confused, but frequently the speaker is also.

Feelings do get buried with the use of this phrase: the phrase fools both the listener and speaker into believing that a feeling or feelings have been revealed, and often there are intense feelings behind the thought or perception that is presented. Thus, feelings get covered up that the speaker needs to reveal and the listener would either like or need to hear. When the above example is carried further, this is usually what happens:

Jack: What are you feeling anxious (guilty, uncomfortable, etc.) about?
Response: I think the group will think I am selfish because I'm taking all the time.
Jack: Well, do you have any kind of evidence that any one of us is thinking that way?
Response: No. But I'm afraid of being rejected if I take too much time.
Jack: Well, I think it would be very important for you to find out what we actually are thinking, don't you?
Response: Yes. [The person then asks each group member what they are thinking about the use of group time. Some

responses to this question are— "If I wanted some time, I'd let you know," or "That thought didn't even cross my mind," or "No, I'm relating to what you are saying."

Jack: Do those responses tell you anything?

Response: Somebody's talking inside my head and making it sound like the members of the group.

If the feelings had not been revealed, the subject would have continued to believe unconsciously in the veracity of what the internal voice was saying to it about its position and value in the group. At some indistinct level, we, as members of the group, would have appeared to be oppressors toward the subject. As a result, both the subject and the group would get a "bad deal."

There is another variation of the same kind of phraseology that plays a slightly different trick on both speaker and listener. An example of that variation would be, "I feel that you are angry with me." To begin with, "I" cannot feel what "you" are feeling. Therefore, this variation confuses things. This is a perfect example of the disappearance of both subject and object from the perspective of the speaker. The subject does not articulate what it is feeling; the object is not consulted as to what it is, in fact, feeling. Therefore, the object-person standing before the subject is merely a mirage created inside the mind of that subject. When I hear this particular sentence (as I frequently do, especially in group process), my response is:

Jack: Well, you can't feel his/her anger, can you?

Response: No.

Jack: Well, what are you feeling, believing that he/she is angry with you?

Response: I feel fear that he/she will reject me.

Jack: I see! Well, don't you think it would be a very good idea to check out with him/her to find out if he/she is actually angry or not? And—even if that turns out to be the case—don't you think it would be wise to find out if his/her anger would entail the rejection of you?

Response: Yeah, I guess I'm basing a lot of feelings on a lot of assumptions.

Jack: Yeah. I would say so.

By giving up the grammatical responsibility for the other person's feeling states and taking responsibility for one's own, one can go a long way to unseat the power of the Inner Other. It can also, I might add, make the interpersonal event much cleaner, trimmer, and more uncomplicated.

There is another common type of sentence that also presumes that the subject is totally responsible for the feeling of the Other. It runs like this: "If I do that, I will make him/her angry." Dana came to one session greatly distressed because she had made a shopping date a week before Christmas with a neighbor with whom she was trying to establish a deeper friendship. She was upset because she would not be able to get a number of tasks finished by Friday, the day of the date. When I asked her why she simply didn't call the woman and postpone the date, she said that she was afraid that she would "make" her friend angry. I responded by saying she could not "make" anyone feel anything. She looked perplexed and said she couldn't understand how I could say that.

I said, "Well, suppose you called up your friend and said: 'Mary, I'm really behind in getting things ready for Christmas. What do you think about us postponing our date until after Christmas?' What if Mary replies by saying: 'Gee, you know, I'm really happy you called because I'm having the same difficulty and that would really be a good idea.'" At that point a very surprised expression came across Dana's face. She said that she never had thought of it that way. I then asked her about her belief that she could "make" someone feel something. She said that this example certainly altered it.

It is true that persons do have emotional reactions to our interactions with them. But our interactions with them are only a small part of their experience of their total environment, personal and impersonal. Mary might have had a different emotional reaction to Dana's proposal if she were not pressured by Christmas plans also. For instance, one reaction could have been disappointment. But Mary's feeling response to Dana's proposal is not just in reference to Dana but to a much broader complex of factors. If Dana (or anyone) believes that she has the power to "make" anyone feel any particular feeling, they are assuming an omnipotence in relation to others that they do not possess.

Although we do not cause or make another feel what they feel, we are a *part* of the overall picture to which they are reacting with their feelings. Therefore, it is important that we listen to what the other is feeling and why it is feeling it. For instance, in the example given, if Dana's friend had said that she was disappointed, this tells Dana that her being with the woman in this activity was important to the woman. Based on that, there is a communication from the woman that the budding relationship is important to her. This then indicates to Dana that this woman has an investment in the budding relationship just as Dana does. If, on the other hand, the woman responds that she is angry about the cancellation because she went ahead, cancelled other plans that were important to her, and made special plans for the day with Dana (lunch, travel arrangements), again knowing this, Dana could reevaluate her own position to see whether it is that important to cancel the day because of the Christmas rush. Given the circumstances, the woman has a legitimate reason for her anger toward Dana. Dana did not cause the anger, but it is in reaction to something that Dana did in the context of the cancellation of her other plans, etc. It is then up to Dana to evaluate what she did and why she needed to do it, and to weigh that against the woman's needs, the frustration to which she is reacting with anger. As they talk, the goal needs to be an increasing understanding of the needs of each so that they can come to some kind of compromise between them that is satisfactory to both.

There is another form of words that can also cause the subject a loss of identity through the dissociation of thoughts and feelings. This vocabulary grouping I label "qualifiers." Examples of these qualifying words and phrases are: I guess, I suppose, perhaps, maybe. The kinds of sentences these qualifiers might be found in would be: "I suppose I was feeling guilty about that" or "I guess I was thinking that I should go." The subject never needs to guess what it is thinking or feeling. Either the subject is thinking or feeling something or it is not. It is possible that a person may not have worked out in its mind a logical sequence so that it can articulate clearly what it is thinking. Or it may be that a person is feeling something or is experiencing a complex of feelings that is hard to identify. In that case, when it is asked what is happening to it internally at either of these two levels, the response can be: "I'm not sure what I'm thinking (feeling)" or "I don't know what I'm feeling (thinking)." In either case, the subject is taking a definite, specific stand about itself in its thinking or feeling states. In that it has an identity.

However, when a person uses the qualifiers, its thinking and feeling states are diluted. These kinds of qualifiers cause the subject to have a sense of vagueness about itself which, in turn, leaves it wide open for the attack of the Inner Other. As we have seen, if the focus on events, whether internal or external, is blurred in nonspecificity, the subject has a great deal of difficulty understanding what and who it is reacting to. It is at this point that the Inner Other can step into the diffuse event and begin superimposing its values and beliefs onto the subject and event at hand.

If, however, the subject watches for these qualifiers and eliminates them from the vocabulary of self-description, it can avoid this pitfall. If the subject does recognize that it *is* feeling (thinking) something and states *that,* in claiming that aspect of its identity it leaves no room for the interpolation of the Inner Other. On the other hand, if the subject comes to identify clearly that it doesn't know precisely what it is thinking (feeling) and states that unequivocally, it is also stating very concretely its state of being, namely a state of being of nonknowledge about itself. This leaves no room for the Inner Other to move in and take over the identity of the subject.

There is a group of verbs that leave the subject wide open to attack and undermining by the Inner Other. I label them the moral-imperative verbs. They are: *should, ought,* and *have to.* When these verbs are used, there is usually some kind of moral imperative implied. It is true there are moral imperatives in the world: "I should not murder other people." "I ought not to run that stop sign because I might be responsible for an accident." In such cases, these verbs are used appropriately. Much of the time, however, these verbs are not used in this appropriate sense. They do, nevertheless, carry with them that "moral" meaning even when they are used inappropriately. For instance:

Dana: I wonder if I should go to that party I was invited to.
Jack: Why *should* you go?

Dana: Well, they invited me and they would be insulted if I didn't accept the invitation.

Jack: True, they might be insulted if you didn't go. Let's assume for the moment that they *would* be insulted if you declined the invitation. That still raises for me the question of the morality of your deciding to go or not to go based on their being insulted. Do you understand what I'm saying?

Dana: Yes, I do. My decision to go or not to go isn't a moral decision. The "should" certainly implies that because I can feel that, but I don't know what else to use.

Jack: Well, what is it you feel if you don't go and they are insulted by that?

Dana: Guilt!

Jack: Exactly! Therein is the "moral" imperative.

Clearly the "morality" was that of the Inner Other: It was Dana's "moral" responsibility to assume the burden of the other person's feeling responses. I tried to help her change the vocabulary she was using and the belief system contained within it.

Jack: Let me propose a different way of asking the same question and see what you come up with. "Do I want to go to the party they invited me to?" Say that question and let's see what happens.

Dana: Do I want to go to the party they invited me to?

Jack: What's the answer to that question?

Dana: The answer is a very clear, "YES!"

Jack: What happened this time around that didn't happen before?

Dana: Well, for one thing all the guilt disappeared. The other thing is that I was asking myself and something else, *they* weren't telling me.

Jack: Why *do* you want to go?

Dana: Because I like the people who invited me. I've been to other parties they've had and I've really enjoyed them. I think I would have a really good time!

Jack: Well, that sounds like good enough reasons to me for wanting to go.

There is another very valuable form of speech that can be helpful in understanding our unconscious processes. Sometimes we will say: "One part of me says . . . but another part of me says. . . ." People do not realize the significance of this because the idiom really means what it says. There *are* two parts that are speaking. The only untruth in the idiom is that one part is not usually the "*me*"; it is the "you" or the Inner Other. Because people do not realize the importance of this form of words, they do not use it to clarify who is speaking, or what feelings are generated by whom. Invariably, when this expression is used, the one part that is speaking is the Inner Other and the other is usually the "Child-I":

Dana: There is a part of me that wants to take advantage of this nice, new spring weather and take the afternoon off and go to the park and sit in the sun. But there is another part of me that tells me to go back to work after I leave here today.
Jack: Well, can you quote what each side says to you? "I say to myself, comma, quotation marks. . . ."
Dana: I say to myself, "I really want to get some sun after that long winter we had. I really need to relax. There's nothing pressing at the office anyway."
Jack: And what does the other part say?
Dana: It says, "You're going to take more time off again? When are you going to learn that you've got responsibilities? If you don't go back this afternoon, what are they going to think about you?"
Jack: Do you hear it?
Dana: I sure do.
Jack: Who's speaking?
Dana: They are. They're trying to take over my life again.
Jack: Who was speaking in the first part?
Dana: That was my Child!
Jack: Who do you want to listen to?
Dana: My Child!
Jack: Why?
Dana: Because she's right, we need today off. There's really nothing to do back at the office today. After all, I am the boss. If I've done my work, why not take the rest of the day off?!
Jack: What will all the rest think of you if you do?
Dana: Who cares?! I'm the boss. That's just my internal bosses carrying on. "Go to hell!"

Once Dana and Chris came to terms with their internal reality and realized its importance, the old, previously unresolvable conflicts became resolvable. As they unlearned the old skills around disowning of the Self and learned the new ones of owning the Self by observing it and the world of objects around it, inside and out, they began to experience new freedom and a sense of identity that had been rare before. They learned that there were very concrete tools they could use to understand the Self-in-the-world: to be aware of their feelings, to understand what they were in reaction to, to judge what was happening that aroused those feelings, and to act on the judgments; and to listen to their vocabulary and grammar in order to move away from the power of the Inner Others and toward self-identity, integrity, and autonomy. They are tools that we all can use to achieve the same life goals, if we choose to do so.

Epilogue

THE END OF THE OLD JOURNEY— THE BEGINNING OF THE NEW

Dana initially sought counseling because of her uncomfortable feelings of anxiety and confusion; her inability to make decisions in her life, even around some of the most mundane matters; and the massive immobility that these things caused her. Through the course of her therapeutic journey, she discovered the roots of her anxiety, indecision, and immobility—the inner personages who robbed her of her identity, autonomy, and integrity as a person. These inner demons replaced her sense of well-being with monumental guilt, anxiety, uncertainty, and powerlessness.

Dana had unwittingly made these Inner Other voices the foundation upon which she based her sense of identity— in fact, the very source of her being. She had come to believe that because of the circumstances of her childhood she could not live without their directives, their judgments, their way of doing things. Therefore, when the Inner Other reality of these voices was pointed out to her, she found it initially impossible to confront them. She began to realize the significance of the "you" addresses from within, as I doggedly pointed out to her the frequency with which they intruded on her conversations, but even when we further examined the burdensome content of what they were saying to her, she still found it very threatening to face up to them and confront them.

Ever since she constructed them during her childhood, they had presented themselves to her as absolutely necessary for her survival. Therefore, the contrary thought of confronting them threatened to plunge her into a deep, dark abyss of chaotic nothingness. However, as she slowly realized that the life they gave her was in reality a living death, she became, ever so tentatively, more willing to question them and to confront their activity inside of her. The threat from them was that she would fall in, if she dared go against what they told her about reality—without them there was no reality.

My function was to be at her side, to help her see that the life these voices offered her was indeed no life at all. To challenge them was not in reality to risk losing anything. In fact, she had everything to gain. As that became clearer to her, I was there to encourage her, even at times to help her formulate the words in which she could confront the Inner Others. As the angry words began to slip out, I stood by her to help her realize she didn't disappear after saying them. Rather, she, in her own experience, became more alive.

As she explored these more overt and conscious acts of rebellion against their internal rule of her, the more covert acts of guerrilla warfare that had previously manifested themselves in the indecision; the chronic and, at times, acute symptoms of vomiting, esophageal collapse, etc.; and the underlying anxiety began to subside. They did, however, reach a plateau below which she seemed unable to go. Along with that was a lingering sense of inner pain and emptiness. That was when we began to search for her inner Child.

As we talked, we did indeed find that deeply buried part of herself that Dana had denied long ago in her childhood. That "Child-I" needed to be claimed back if her healing was to be complete. However, when Dana started talking with that disowned part of herself, this unleashed a new frontal attack by her inner tormentors.

Again, though, I stood with her, encouraged her conversation with her Girl while she pushed away the Inner Others. She found that, if she had faith in herself and that long lost part of herself, she came alive even more radically than she had before. True, to give up the Inner Others initially seemed to be choosing death—because to give them up seemed to be giving up her last, tenuous hold on life. This, of course, caused her to cling all the more closely to them.

With the encouragement that I and the members of the group were able to provide her, she repeatedly took leaps of faith in which she both let go of the demons and grasped her Child. She could then also recognize the true reality of who we were as persons—and not the menacing mirages her Inner Others made us into. She *did* face death, but it was the death of them and not of herself—so she found out. The result was that *she* rose from *their* ashes. Each time she confronted them, claimed her Child and the real outside world of persons, she struck another blow against their control.

I had taught her all I could about the activity of the Inner Others and what it meant in the loss of her identity; I had explored with her the significance of her Girl and the importance of listening for who the real External Other was. Dana knew well their words and phrases. Her success at hearing them when they spoke and confronting them when they did so had begun to become automatic. Our task together was over. Our goals had been achieved: Dana now knew who her oppressors were, and she knew what to do when they appeared on the scene. It was time for us to say goodbye. Her therapeutic journey was over. She did not need me any longer.

Dana summed up her new life in the following words:

> I'm taking more opportunity of getting out into the world, which is something I'm not famous for, and I'm looking forward to it, not with any of the old trepidation. I go out into the world and take what pleasure there is there. If there are any things that are not terrific, I pass on. They are not going to make the sun rise or fall. Not everything is so dire. Everything was such a Greek *tragedy.* [Laughing] It didn't happen to anyone else like it happened to *me*! In neon lights! You know, every event in my life was something you could write a play about. That's such a crock. I mean life is . . . up and down, sweet and sour, and all the rest of it. And on you go. And on *I* go. I get pleasure right now out of very ordinary things. The ordinary things in life that I never used to think were important. It had to be super anxious for it to be exciting and therefore to be worthwhile. And now I find the calm parts of life to be the easy parts, not the big, eventful things but the ordinary things in life, the comfortable things in life. That's my key word now in life, I really love the word comfortable, comfort—the lacking in anxiety. And it's amazing that the things

that I used to think were so scary before are really not so. That was my own doing in conjunction with my sweet Mother, Aunt and Father. Once I shook off that real influence that I felt from them, then the things that used to have anxiety became life-size. They were ordinary things. I can handle everything. I can *really* do it. And I don't have to question myself. Yeah, there are some things I'm going to make a mistake with. I love the fact that I own up to mistakes. I used to go wild, I used to lie like crazy years ago to hide out from. . . . "They'll find out that I did that wrong." And now I sort of own up and I say, "Hey, I really screwed that one up." "You know that's really funny, I screwed it up." And nobody kills me and nobody hates me or rejects me. They laugh and say, "You know, I did that too" or "So what? So let's go on." I'm learning that the imperfect doesn't mean "bad." It means "human." And therefore there's not a lot of my value hanging on a mistake. I stop killing myself. Which is what I was doing before. Or at least I stopped joining her and *them* in killing me. I guess that's how it is now. It's ordinary—life-size.

As Dana had learned to let go of her Internal Parents and claim her "Child-I," Chris learned to walk away from his very powerful Internal Mother and to claim his deeply alienated and hurting Little Boy. As he accomplished those tasks, he also discovered that the world out there loved and valued him.

Chris summed up his new life this way:

Really listening for me requires being very active. And that keeps me out of my own stuff. So it makes me more comfortable because I'm not involved in all the swirling stuff that I could easily get involved in. It gets me away from my Internal Mother and gets me out into the world. I think that is the most important thing for me. The second thing is to be able to take in what I hear and not so readily to process it through my very negative inner voices, but to try to accept it as the truth no matter what my Internal Mother says. I've learned that, when she says it is good, it is not true and when she says it is bad it *is* true. [He laughs.] Certainly I take all those things with me outside. It makes me a more effective debater because in a way that is what my Child is all about. I'm really listening to what the Child is saying. It has taught me to ask questions and to be less afraid of appearing stupid because my Internal Mother says, "Well, you stupid, you can't ask a dumb question like that." But if I'm dealing with

> reality, of course I can ask a question like that. There's no judgment to any question. There are some people who like to make it that, and I run into them on occasion. But if I'm dealing out there and not in here [points to his head], I can respond to the issue. If someone were to say to me, "Well, that's a dumb question," I can say something like, "Well, there's no such thing as a dumb question" or "Yeah. Well, could you give me the answer anyhow?" And if I don't take that and make that a judgment on me, I can just deal with whatever the issue is and whatever they say. That makes me a more effective person. Also it makes me less afraid. I don't spend my life afraid all the time. My Child is afraid at times. But I comfort that Child. It doesn't always work right away and my Internal Mother doesn't always get out of there right away. But over the long haul it seems to be lessening, my voice, that is. And I seem to be getting more of myself. And I don't see other people as "the enemy" any more.

He had come to realize that the world out there was not one of adversaries and enemies but one that could be loving and caring. Part of learning this was learning to stop listening to his Internal Mother, who made others appear to be what they weren't. As he gave her up, he became more comfortable with the world. Because he could now trust, he didn't have to be so lonely—and he wasn't.

This is not to say that Dana's or Chris's Inner Others were dead. They weren't. Nor do I believe they will ever die or disappear. Certainly, they were no longer in control of either of these two persons. Rather, Dana and Chris were now mainly in charge of their own lives.

Further, it would be erroneous to believe that the Inner Others would never raise their ugly heads and either attempt to take over or in fact do so, for they would and did. Through the therapeutic process Dana and Chris now knew what to do when their Inner Others became active. What had been a lifetime of slavery now needed only to be a momentary struggle or at worst several hours or days of scuffling for power. Occasionally Dana and Chris have called to see me for a session to help get some clarity when they found themselves in some especially stressful situation. Their lives have been ones, though, of greater happiness, as well as power and control over themselves.

I would like to say to them then, "Fight the good fight, Dana and Chris. Claim what is yours to claim. I'm happy to have been with you in your battle and to have been of aid to you in your victory. I am with you in spirit as you continue toward clarity and your personal integrity."